CEFR A2-B1

B

FRAMEWORK ENGLISH

Tim Woolstencroft   Colin Thompson

KINSEIDO

Kinseido Publishing Co., Ltd.
3-21 Kanda Jimbo-cho, Chiyoda-ku,
Tokyo 101-0051, Japan

First published 2024 by Kinseido Publishing Co., Ltd.

Design: DAITECH co., ltd.

Acknowledgements

The authors would like to thank the students, teachers and staff at Josai International University for their help during the writing and piloting of Framework English series. In particular, we would like to thank Dr. Kenji Sugibayashi and professor Masato Kurabayashi for their continued support of this project.

A huge debt of thanks is owed to Professor Maria Shiguemi Ichiyama for her invaluable advice and support.

Finally, we would like to express our sincerest thanks to Nobuko Ito and Yukiko Thompson, who provided inspiration, cultural help and language support, not to mention unstinting patience.

CEFR-J wordlist - The CEFR-J Wordlist Version 1.6. Compiled by Yukio Tono, Tokyo University of Foreign Studies. Retrieved from http://www.cefrj.org/download.html#cefrj_wordlist on 01/09/2023.

 音声ファイル無料ダウンロード

https://www.kinsei-do.co.jp/download/4201

この教科書で 🎧 DL 00 の表示がある箇所の音声は、上記 URL または QR コードにて
無料でダウンロードできます。自習用音声としてご活用ください。

▶ PC からのダウンロードをお勧めします。スマートフォンなどでダウンロードされる場合は、
　ダウンロード前に「解凍アプリ」をインストールしてください。
▶ URL は、検索ボックスではなくアドレスバー (URL 表示欄) に入力してください。
▶ お使いのネットワーク環境によっては、ダウンロードできない場合があります。

◎ CD 00　左記の表示がある箇所の音声は、教室用 CD (Class Audio CD) に収録されています。

Introduction

Welcome to *Framework English B*. This is book 2 in a series of English language textbooks designed to improve learners' communicative and cognitive skills. Based on the aims and assessment criteria of the Common European Framework of Reference for Languages (CEFR), this book follows CEFR's goals for developing learners' language skills. CEFR's assessment criteria is categorized into proficiency levels (A1-C2), and this action-based book primarily targets A2-B1 levels. Vocabulary has been selected largely from the A2-B2 CEFR-J levels; a CEFR informed word list designed for Asian learners of English. Book 2 builds on book 1 by targeting higher levels of CEFR-J rated vocabulary and CEFR rated grammar. The selected language has been allocated within 6 topic-based modules of personal, social, educational and professional relevance for learners, by covering topics such as biographies, personalities and predictions. In doing so, learners can develop interpersonal and intrapersonal skills by understanding how people can communicate effectively, as well as knowing their own strengths and weaknesses, and identifying their potential career paths. Furthermore, these modules are looked at from international viewpoints so learners can improve their understanding of multiculturalism and express their opinions about different cultures.

Each module follows a systematic structure. Learners are first provided with learning goals, followed by a progression of tasks and activities that allow learners to practice and develop communicative and cognitive skills. Each module also provides visual graphic organizers that help learners to extract key information from complex listening and reading texts. Graphic organizers are also used to help students develop strategies for planning and organizing their thoughts clearly for productive writing. At the end of each module, learners complete "Can-do" statements which reflect the goals outlined at the start of the module, enabling them to assess their strengths and weaknesses. There are also three review units that consist of research projects where learners answer research questions by collecting and reporting on data using key language features of the modules. In doing so, learners develop important cognitive skills such as analyzing information, reasoning, inferring, and displaying visual data.

The communicative and cognitive skills developed from using *Framework English B* can benefit life-long learning not only in relation to students' English studies, but also other areas of their academic studies, as well as their future careers.

C O N T E N T S

MODULE Outline *Using Framework English B*

Goals Introduces the module and activates learners' L2 resources.

1st Unit   *Unit 1, 3, 6, 8, 11, 13*

MATCH — Learners complete a picture matching task.

SCAN — Learners practice scanning for information.

FOCUS — Learners focus on communicative functions.

LISTEN — Learners practice their listening skills by completing picture matching tasks, written texts, as well as organizing and summarizing key information using graphic organizers.

COMMUNICATE — Learners practice their communication skills by completing tasks and activities that use the target language.

2nd Unit   *Unit 2, 4, 7, 9, 12, 14*

READ — Learners engage in pre-reading activities to activate their topic knowledge, then practice reading topic-based texts, before organizing and summarizing key information using graphic organizers.

WRITE — Learners develop different writing skills by engaging in vocabulary, grammar and skills-based exercises.

VOCABULARY — Learners test their knowledge of topic-based CEFR-J vocabulary (A2 - B1 - B2 - + (No level), by completing vocabulary activities and a crossword..

LANGUAGE REVIEW — Learners review selected grammar and vocabulary items by completing a series of language exercises.

Self-Check Learners evaluate their knowledge and skills learned from each module using CEFR related can-do descriptors.

Review   *Unit 5, 10, 15*

After completing two modules, learners engage in communicative, research-based projects using key vocabulary from the modules.

MODULE 1

Biographies

GOALS:

 Can you scan for information about people's biographies?

 Can you ask and answer personal questions?

 Can you understand a conversation about studying abroad?

 Can you ask and answer questions about people's backgrounds?

 Can you understand a biography of a famous person?

 Can you write your own biography ?

 Can you understand vocabulary related to biographies?

MATCH

Match the people in photographs **1-5** with mini resumes **a ~ e** below.

1.
2.
3.
4.
5.

a
Age: 23
Name: Jane Macdonald
Nationality: American
Education: New York
   University, BA
University Major:

Work experience: Sound
   engineer, DJ
Interests: Music

b
Age: 26
Name: Daniel Martinez
Nationality: Mexican
Education: University of
   Mexico, B. Med
University Major:

Work experience: Dental
   assistant
Interests: Jogging

c
Age: 27
Name: Felicia Gunawan
Nationality: Indonesian
Education: State
   University of Jakarta, BA
University Major:

Work experience: Resort
   hotel staff
Interests: Cooking

d
Age: 24
Name: Duncan Jones
Nationality: New
   Zealander
Education: University of
   North Auckland, BA
University Major:

Work experience: Bank
   internship
Interests: Traveling

e
Age: 25
Name: Angela Reyes
Nationality: Filipino
Education: University of
   the Philippines, BA
University Major:

Work experience:
   Physical therapist
Interests: Visiting art
   museums & galleries

SCAN

What are their majors?

A *Scanning for information:* <u>In 4 minutes</u>, scan the texts below to find the key information. Check your answers on the previous page.

B Read the texts again and add the correct university majors to the mini resumes on the previous page.

 DL 02   CD 02

1.  I grew up surrounded by music in New Orleans. Both of my parents are musicians and I love all kinds of music. I enjoy making my own music in my free time, so I decided to major in Media Studies. While I was at university in New York, I regularly used to DJ at a club. After graduation, I got a job working as a sound engineer in a music studio. I absolutely love my job and still have a real passion for music and music production.

2. I'm so lucky. I live and work on the paradise island of Bali. I studied Tourism Management at university in Jakarta. After graduation, I worked in a hotel there for five years. I love the career I have chosen, but it can be tiring. You need to be a very polite, sociable and outgoing person. I enjoy cooking after work, and one of the chefs at the hotel is teaching me some new recipes.

3.  At high school, my favorite subjects were math, physics and chemistry. I was the class president and worked as a volunteer in my local community. After I graduated, I took a gap year and traveled around South America. I studied Spanish at school in New Zealand, which helped me learn more about the culture there. I graduated from university with a degree in Economics and I now have an internship at a large bank in Tokyo.

4. I used to work as a dental assistant but I decided to go back to school and I saved enough money to study for a university degree. I am now majoring in Medicine. It has always been my dream to become a doctor. I'm currently living with my parents in Mexico City, as this helps me save money. I'm hoping to graduate next year. I don't have a lot of free time, but I go jogging in the evenings. It helps me keep fit.

5.  I was born and raised in the Philippines. My favorite subject at high school was PE, and I belonged to both the basketball team and the swimming team. I majored in Physical Therapy at a university in Manila and found a job as a physical therapist in a hospital there after I graduated. I really love painting in my free time. It's very relaxing and I often go to art exhibitions at local museums and galleries.

C In pairs, discuss with your partner which of the people above are most similar to you and whose career path you would most like to follow.

Asking and answering personal questions

A *Personal information:* Match phrases **1-6** with pictures **a-f** below.

1. Yes, I work in a restaurant. · · · · · · · · ☐

2. I'm studying Journalism. · · · · · · · · · · ☐

3. I was born in Tokyo. · · · · · · · · · · · · ☐

4. I'm into music, especially J-pop. · · · · ☐

5. I want to be a movie director. · · · · · · · ☐

6. I belonged to the soccer club. · · · · · · ☐

a.

b.

c.

d.

e.

f.

B *Personal questions:* Match questions **7-12** with phrases **1-6**.

7. Where were you born? · · · · · · · · · · · · ☐

8. What's your major? · · · · · · · · · · · · · · ☐

9. What are your interests? · · · · · · · · · · · ☐

10. What school clubs did you belong to? · · ☐

11. Do you have a part-time job? · · · · · · · · ☐

12. What do you want to do in the future? ☐

C 💬💬 *Let's talk:* In pairs, practice interviewing your partner using questions **7-12**.

D *Describe your partner:* Write about your partner, then practice describing them.

My partner's name is _____. She/He was born in _____.

_____

_____

_____

_____

_____

_____

LISTEN   **Study abroad conversation**

 DL 03   CD 03

A Listen to the first part of a conversation with a student who is studying abroad. Write the person's name in the box and put a check mark (✓) in the correct circles.

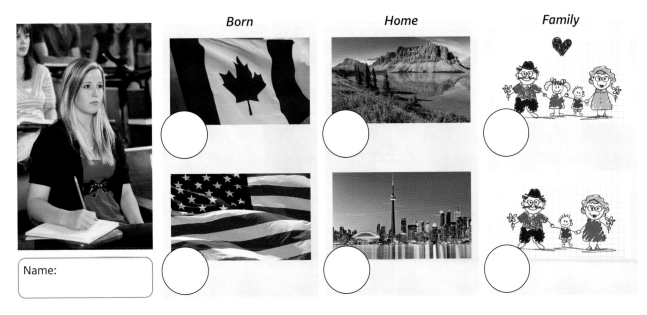

Name:

Born   Home   Family

B Read the conversation below and try to guess the missing words. Then listen to the conversation again, check your answers and complete it.

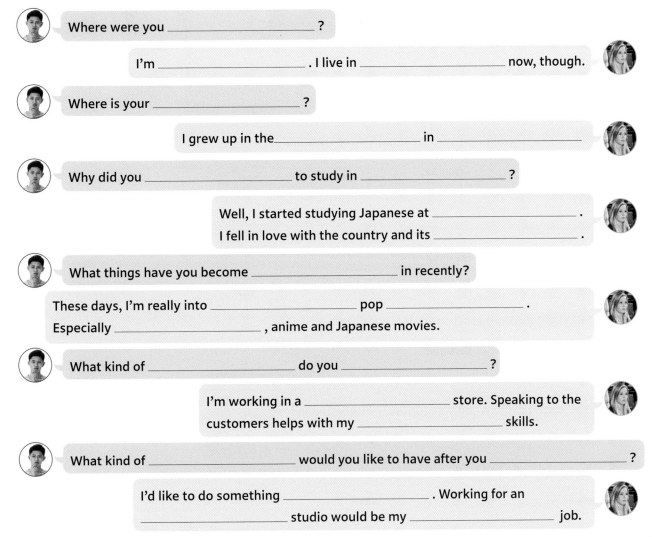

Where were you _____?

I'm _____ . I live in _____ now, though.

Where is your _____?

I grew up in the_____ in _____

Why did you _____ to study in _____?

Well, I started studying Japanese at _____ .
I fell in love with the country and its _____ .

What things have you become _____ in recently?

These days, I'm really into _____ pop _____ .
Especially _____ , anime and Japanese movies.

What kind of _____ do you _____?

I'm working in a _____ store. Speaking to the
customers helps with my _____ skills.

What kind of _____ would you like to have after you _____?

I'd like to do something _____ . Working for an
_____ studio would be my _____ job.

C Listen to the whole conversation and put a check mark (✓) in the picture Ⓐ or Ⓑ that matches the content.

Ⓐ   Ⓑ

1. Born & grew up

2. School club

3. University — Alberta / Seattle

4. Part-time job

5. Current interest

6. Dream job

D 💬💬 Give your opinion!

1. I would like to work in my home region after I graduate.

Agree: _____ Disagree: _____

Why? _____

2. It is important to belong to a club at school.

Agree: _____ Disagree: _____

Why? _____

3. Working in a convenience store is a good part-time job.

Agree: _____ Disagree: _____

Why? _____

4. What kinds of things are you currently interested in?

Answer: _____ Why? _____

5. What would you like to do after you graduate from university?

Answer: _____ Why? _____

COMMUNICATE   Who are you most similar to?

Interview members of your class to find people who are similar to you. First, complete questions **1-10** in the table below and write your answers. Then ask the same questions to the other members of the class.

If **the 1st person** you ask has the same answer as you = **5 points**
2nd person = **4 points** **3rd person** = **3 points**
4th person = **2 points** **5th person** = **1 point**
If **nobody** has the same answer as you after asking 5 people = **0 points**

	Find someone who...	Your answer	Name of the person with the same answer	Points
1.	... was born in the same prefecture as you. Q: *Where were you born?*			
2.	... was born in the same month as you. Q:			
3.	... likes the same kind of music as you. Q:			
4.	... belonged to the same club at school. Q:			
5.	... enjoys doing the same thing in their free time. Q:			
6.	... had the same favorite subject at high school. Q:			
7.	... wants to do the same kind of job after they graduate. Q:			
8.	... has done the same kind of part-time job as you. Q:			
9.	... has been to the same number of countries as you. Q:			
10.	... is into the same _____ as you. Q:			

TOTAL points

READ

What's my name?

Name

[   ]

A Look at the picture of the famous person above. If you know his name, write it in the space above. Read the questions below and try to answer them. If you don't know the answers, try to guess the correct answer. Read the biography on the next page and check the correct answers.

1. When was he born?
   a 1879 **b** 1909 **c** 1919

2. Where was he born?
   a Germany **b** Israel **c** USA

3. Where did he go to college?
   a Berlin **b** London **c** Zurich

4. What was his major at college?
   a Physics and math **b** Chemistry **c** Biology

5. When did he win the Nobel Prize?
   a 1911 **b** 1921 **c** 1931

6. How many children did he have?
   a None **b** One **c** Two

7. How many times was he married?
   a Once **b** Twice **c** Three times

8. When did he die?
   a 1945 **b** 1955 **c** 1965

B Read the biography again and complete the timeline below with information about his life.

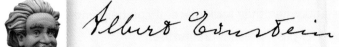

Albert Einstein was born on 14 March, 1879 in Germany. He had a younger sister called Maja. He didn't like school and was only an average student, however he had a great mind for math and physics. When he was 15, his family moved to Milan in Italy for work. After this, he moved to Switzerland to attend school and college in Zurich. In 1900 he graduated with a degree in physics and math. After graduation, he took an office job in Bern, Switzerland. In his free time, he began to work on his own theories.

In 1903, he married his college mate Mileva Maric, and one year later Einstein's first son, Hans Albert, was born. His second son Eduard followed in 1910. He worked as a university professor in both Zurich and Prague, before becoming the director of a new research institute in Berlin in 1914.

In 1915, he completed his 'theory of relativity' and the equation he made famous, $e=mc^2$. Einstein got divorced from his wife Mileva and shortly after married his cousin Elsa Löwenthal in 1919. The same year, an experiment proved his theory was correct, and he became world famous. He was awarded the Nobel Prize for Physics in 1921.

Einstein was Jewish, and he left Germany in December 1932 to escape Hitler and the Nazis. In 1933, he moved to the USA, never returning to Germany. In December 1936, Einstein's wife Elsa died, and on April 18 1955, Albert Einstein died from heart failure. He was 76 years old.

	14 March 1879	Born in Germany
	1894	
	1900	
	1903	
	1914	
	1915	
	1919	
	1921	
	1933	
	18 April 1955	

Your story

A A timeline is a way to understand events, dates and when they took place. It can help you plan your writing in order to explain a series of events from the past, present and future.

Read Tom's timeline, then complete his biography below using the information in the timeline.

			← PAST		PRESENT	FUTURE →
2004	2009	2014	2014	2023	Now	??
Born	Started elementary School	Moved to Liverpool	Started high school	Started University (Medicine)	Working part-time	Graduate university
					Play for university soccer club	Work at a hospital
						Work abroad

Tom

I _____ born in Dublin, Ireland in 2004. I _____ elementary school in 2009. When I was _____ , I moved to Liverpool, England, before I started high school. I _____ soccer in my high school team for 3 years.

Since 2023, I've been a student at a university in Manchester. My _____ is Medicine. These days, I'm _____ part-time at a convenience store. I also _____ to the university soccer team.

After I graduate from university, I'm going to _____ for a job at a hospital in London. I'd also like to work _____ in the future.

B Make a timeline about your life. List important events from your past, your interests and things you are doing now, as well as the job you would like after you graduate and your goals for the future.

← PAST	PRESENT	FUTURE →
•	•	•
•	•	•
•	•	•
•	•	•
•	•	•

C Write about your biography using the examples and details from the timeline above.

What's your story?

VOCABULARY

Adjectives

average A2	....
current B1	....
dental B2	....
divorced B1	....
fit A2	....
lucky A1	....
part-time B1	....
polite A2	....
private A2	....
similar A2	....
tiring B1	....

Adverbs

abroad A2	....
absolutely B1	....
currently B1	....
especially A2	....

recently A2	....
regularly A2	....

Nouns

assistant B1	....
business A1	....
career B1	....
chemistry B1	....
communication A2	....
....	
community B2	....
convenience B1 store A1	....
....	
customer A2	....
countryside A2	....
degree A2	....
dream A1	....
economics B1	....

education A2	....
equation B2	....
exhibition A2	....
experience A2	....
gallery A2	....
graduation B1	....
interest A2	....
major B2	....
math A1	....
media B2	....
medicine A1	....
museum A2	....
music A1 production A2	....
....	
passion B1	....
physical A2 therapy B2	....
....	
physics B1	....

president B1	....
recipe B2	....
region B1	....
sound A2 engineer A1	....
....	
theory B1	....
tourism B1	....
volunteer B2	....

Verbs

attend B1	....
belong A2	....
escape B1	....
graduate A2	....
grow A1 up⁺	....
raise A2	....
surround B1	....
volunteer B1	....

A Match each definition with the words on the right.

1. Something that makes you feel that you have no energy: _____
2. A display of items such as works of art: _____
3. An area that is away from big towns and cities: _____
4. Someone who works to help other people without being paid: _____

a. exhibition
b. volunteer
c. tiring
d. countryside

B Fill in the blanks using words that often go with the words in the list.

• dental   _assistant_
• music   _____
• convenience   _____
• sound   _____
• business   _____

C Choose words from the box that best complete the questions. Answer the questions.

dream   graduate   relaxing   currently   grow up

1. What are you planning to do after you [_____]?   A: _____
2. Do you [_____] have a part-time job?   A: _____
3. What free-time activities do you find [_____]?   A: _____
4. What is your [_____] job?   A: _____
5. Did you [_____] in the countryside?   A: _____

D *Crossword:* Complete the crossword using the hints below.

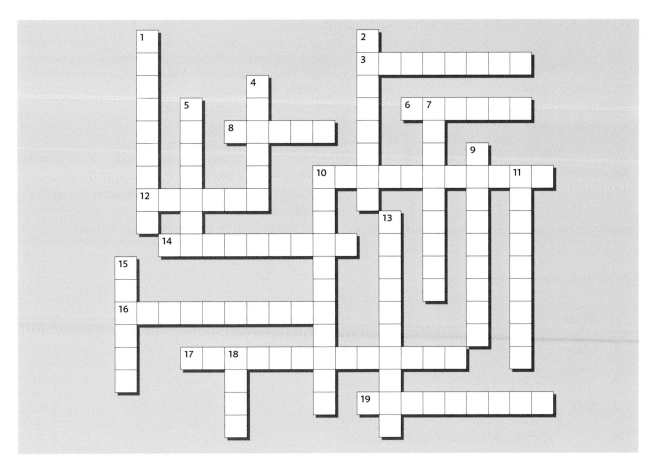

Across

3. My sister is studying Media at university. Her dream is to be a sound _____ .

6.   **8.**

10.  _____ store

12. I was born and _____ in Okinawa. I love living by the sea.

14. My job is to help the dentist. I'm a dental _____ .

16. I'm into all kinds of music, _____ K-pop.

17. Discussions with my classmates help with my _____ skills.

19. In my free time, I often work as a _____ to help my local community.

Down

1.   **2.** I'm majoring in _____ because I want to be a doctor in the future.

4. I'm going to study _____ next year. I'm interested in learning more about foreign cultures.

5.   **7.**

9. I'm trying to keep fit, so I _____ go to the gym.

10.   **11.** I'm _____ living in a small apartment near the university, but I'm hoping to move to a bigger place soon.

13.

15. Einstein discovered the _____ of relativity.   **18.**

LANGUAGE REVIEW

Asking questions to find out biographical information.

Present tense questions (Be verb)	Present tense questions (Other verbs)
Where **are** you from?	Where **do** you **live**?
When **is** your birthday?	What languages **do** you **speak**?
Are you Japanese?	**Do** you **like** Chinese food?

Past tense questions (Be verb)	Past tense questions (Other verbs)
Where **were** your parents born?	Where **did** you **grow up**?
What **was** your favorite subject at school?	What TV programs **did** you **watch** when you were a child?
Were you good at sports when you were a child?	**Did** you **belong** to any clubs at high school?

A Complete the questions below.

1. When _____ you born?   [   ]

2. When _____ you start studying English?   [   ]

3. _____ you have a driving license?   [   ]

4. What _____ your star sign?   [   ]

5. _____ your English teacher from America?   [   ]

6. _____ you eat out last night?   [   ]

7. What _____ you do?   [   ]

8. Who _____ your favorite singer when you were in junior high school?   [   ]

9. _____ you see any good movies last month?   [   ]

10. _____ you interested in baseball?   [   ]

B Match the answers below with the questions above.

a. Leo, my birthday is in August.

b. Not really. I don't really like sports so much.

c. I'm a university student. I'm majoring in Business.

d. No, I haven't been out at all lately. I've been too busy working.

e. Yes I did. I went to a great Italian restaurant near the station.

f. No, not yet. But I'm taking my driving test next summer.

g. I liked Arashi a lot in my early teens. I always used to sing their songs when I went to karaoke.

h. No, she's Australian. I think she's from Perth.

i. About 7 years ago, when I was a junior high school student.

j. I'm sorry that's private. I am over 21, though.

C Now, ask your partner the questions in A.

MODULE 1 SELF-CHECK

Write a score (1-5)* in the boxes below to show how well you can do each part of the module. If you can't do any part well, go back to the page and practice again.

* **1 :** Not at all   **2 :** A little   **3 :** OK   **4 :** Well   **5 :** Very well

UNIT 1

SCAN
I can scan for information about people's biographies (p.7). ·······················

FOCUS
I can ask and answer personal questions (p.8). ·······························

LISTEN
I can understand a conversation about studying abroad (p.9-10). ·············

COMMUNICATE
I can ask and answer detailed personal questions (p.11). ·····················

UNIT 2

READ
I can understand a biography about Albert Einstein (p.12-13) ················

WRITE
I can write my own biography (p.14-15). ·····································

VOCABULARY
I can understand vocabulary related to biographies (p.16-17). ··············

MODULE 2

Personalities

GOALS:

 Can you scan for information about people's personalities?

 Can you ask and answer questions about likes, dislikes, abilities and personalities?

 Can you understand a job interview for a flight attendant?

 Can you answer detailed questions about likes and abilities?

Can you read and understand information about star signs?

Can you write about your likes, dislikes, abilities and personality?

Can you understand vocabulary related to personalities?

MATCH

First, write the names and occupations of the famous people **1-6** from the list below. Then guess the blood type of each famous person.

1.

name: _____

job: _____ blood type: ☐

2.

name: _____

job: _____ blood type: ☐

3.

name: _____

job: _____ blood type: ☐

4.

name: _____

job: _____ blood type: ☐

5.

name: _____

job: _____ blood type: ☐

6.

name: _____

job: _____ blood type: ☐

| *name* | Chiaki Mukai | John Lennon | Pelé | Natsume Soseki | Elizabeth II | Barack Obama |

| *job* | Musican | Queen | Writer | Astronaut | Soccer player | Politician |

blood type	A	O	B	AB
	Kind organizers	*Optimistic leaders*	*Creative rule breakers*	*Unpredictable dreamers*
POSITIVE	intelligent, hardworking, perfectionists	loyal, caring, imaginative	artistic, outgoing, passionate	calm, curious, charming
NEGATIVE	self-centered, too sensitive, easily stressed	jealous, often late, too relaxed and easygoing	wild, irresponsible, easily bored	complicated, moody, insecure

SCAN

What are their blood types?

A *Scanning for information:* <u>In 4 minutes</u>, scan the texts below to find the key information. Check your answers on the previous page.

 DL 07   CD 07

B Read the texts again and highlight the personality adjectives that match the blood type of the famous people below.

1.
Nastume Sōseki was a Japanese novelist. He is well known around the world for the novels he wrote, like *Kokoro*, *Botchan* and *I Am a Cat*. He was born in Tokyo, Japan. He graduated from the University of Tokyo, and at first he became a school teacher. Many people think he was the greatest writer in recent Japanese history. He had blood type A. Although a wonderful writer, Sōseki was also self-centered, easily stressed and often depressed.

2. **Elizabeth II**, born 21 April, 1926, was Queen of the United Kingdom from 1952 until she died on 8 September 2022. Elizabeth was married Prince Philip, who died in 2021. Together, they had four children, eight grandchildren and 12 great-grandchildren. Her eldest son became King Charles III when she died. Her blood type was O. She cared a lot about her role as queen and about her family. She was optimistic and had a relaxed sense of humor.

3.
Barack Obama was the first African-American president of the United States. He was president from 2009 to 2017 and won the Nobel Prize for Peace in 2009. He was born in Hawaii on August 4, 1961 to an American mother and a Kenyan father. He grew up in Jakarta, Indonesia before returning to America and studying Law at university. Known for being calm, charming, and highly intelligent, like many people with AB blood type.

4. **John Lennon** was born in Liverpool, UK, on October 9, 1940. He became world-famous as a singer and guitarist with the Beatles, and for the amazing songs he wrote with Paul McCartney. He was killed in front of his apartment in New York in 1980 at the age of 40. He had two children and was married to Yoko Ono, his second wife, when he died. With O blood type, he had an easygoing, imaginative personality and was loyal to friends and family. He could be jealous at times.

5.
Chiaki Mukai is a Japanese physician and JAXA astronaut, born on May 6, 1952 in Tatebayashi, Gunma Prefecture. She was the first Japanese woman in space. She is very intelligent, graduating from Keio Girls Senior High School in Tokyo, and receiving her doctorate in medicine from Keio University School of Medicine in 1977. She is very ambitious, hardworking and never gives up her dreams. As with other A blood types, she is also a perfectionist.

6. **Edson Arantes do Nascimento**, known as **Pelé**, was born on October 23, 1940, in Brazil. He had B blood type. Many think he was the greatest soccer player of all time. With Pelé, Brazil won the World Cup in 1958 (when he was only 17 years old), 1962 and 1970. After retiring, Pelé composed music, wrote books about his life, and served as Brazil's minister of sports. He died on December 29, 2022. Famous for his speed and skill on the soccer pitch, he had an outgoing and creative nature.

C In pairs, discuss whether or not your personalities match your blood type.

FOCUS

Likes, dislikes, abilities and personalities

A *Personalities:* Match personality adjectives **a-h** with pictures **1-8** below.

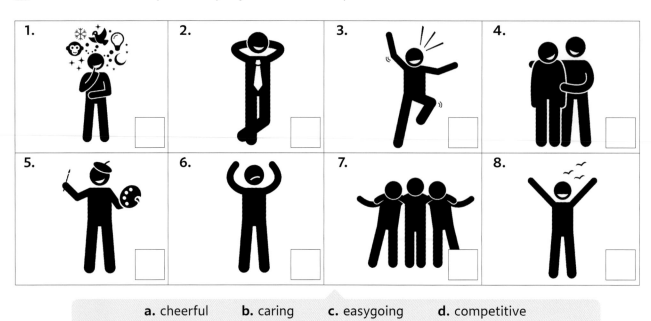

1.	2.	3.	4.
5.	6.	7.	8.

a. cheerful **b.** caring **c.** easygoing **d.** competitive
e. artistic **f.** sociable **g.** energetic **h.** imaginative

B *Likes, dislikes and abilities:* Match the definitions with personality adjectives **a-h**.

	Someone who enjoys playing games and sports. They love winning and hate losing.		A kind person who likes helping others and is good at looking after other people.
	A friendly person who enjoys meeting and talking with other people.		Someone who is creative and is good at drawing and painting.
	Someone who is good at thinking of new and interesting ideas.		A person who likes laughing, joking and is good at making others happy.
	A relaxed person who doesn't get worried or annoyed easily. Good at staying calm.		Someone who is very active and doesn't get tired easily. Enjoys physical activity.

C 💬💬 *Let's talk:* With your partner, ask and answer questions about likes, dislikes, abilities and personalities.

For example:

Do you enjoy playing games?	>	Yes, I really enjoy playing video games. I'm into playing RPG at the moment.
Are you good at playing sports?	>	Yes, quite good. I belonged to the badminton club when I was at high school, but I don't play sports so often these days.
Do you think you are competitive?	>	No , I don't think so. I don't really care about winning or losing. I just enjoy playing games.

LISTEN

 DL 08   CD 08

A Listen to the first part of the job interview. Write the person's name in the box put a check mark (✓) in the correct circles.

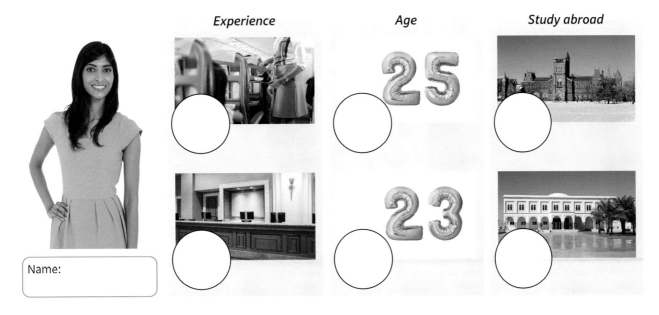

Experience   Age   Study abroad

Name:

 DL 09   CD 09

B Read the continued interview below and try to guess the missing words. Then listen to the conversation, check your answers and complete it below.

 OK, and what do you do there?

I help _____ with their hotel reservations and provide _____ with their stay at the hotel.

 Do you like your job?

Yes, I really like it. I _____ helping people.

 I see, well working at a hotel is good experience for this position. Can you speak any languages?

Yes, I can. Of course, I can speak Hindi. I can also speak English and I'm _____ good at speaking Chinese. I've been _____ Chinese for about 3 years now.

 That's good. And how would you describe your personality?

Well, I'm outgoing and _____. I like meeting my friends. I'm also hardworking (sometimes too hardworking). I'm very _____. I always do my work on time. My friends say I'm not good at relaxing and I wish I was more _____.

C Listen to the rest of the interview. Complete the chart below giving details about the candidate's likes, dislikes, abilities and personality.

LIKES	DISLIKES
helping people,	

GOOD AT	NOT GOOD AT
	relaxing,

PERSONALITY (Positive)	PERSONALITY (Negative)
outgoing,	

D 💬💬 Give your opinion!

1. It is a good idea for students to study abroad while at university.

Agree: _____   Disagree: _____

Why? _____

2. Being sociable is an important skill for a flight attendant.

Agree: _____   Disagree: _____

Why? _____

3. I am hardworking and organized.

Agree: _____   Disagree: _____

Why? _____

4. I am interested in becoming a flight attendant.

Agree: _____   Disagree: _____

Why? _____

5. How would you describe your personality?

Answer: _____

COMMUNICATE

What your interests say about you

Interview your partner (B) asking questions **1-15** in the table below. Check the examples below, then write a score for your partner's answers on a scale of **0-4**.

Do you like/enjoy speaking English? Are you interested in speaking English?	Are you good at speaking English?
-- Yes, I love/really like speaking English. ➡4 points -- Yes, I like speaking English. ➡3 points -- I don't mind speaking English. / It's OK. ➡2 points -- No, I don't (really) like speaking English. ➡1 point -- No, I can't stand/hate speaking English. ➡0 points	-- Yes, I'm really good at speaking English. ➡4 points -- Yes, I'm pretty good at speaking English. ➡3 points -- I'm not bad at speaking English or I'm OK at speaking English. ➡2 points -- No, I'm not very good at speaking English. ➡1 point -- No, I'm terrible/awful at speaking English. ➡0 points

Add the points for each section and write the total in the box. Check the results page(p.29) and read the information in the group that has the highest points total.

Question	RATE					TOTAL
	4	3	2	1	0	
1. Do you like dancing?						
2. Do you enjoy making or fixing things?						
3. Are you good at playing musical instruments?						points
4. Do you like performing in front of people?						
5. Are you good at public speaking?						
6. Do you like wearing unusual or unique clothes?						points
7. Do you enjoy talking to strangers?						
8. Are you interested in doing volunteer work?						
9. Are you good at cooking and doing housework?						points
10. Do you like exercising and keeping fit?						
11. Are you good at swimming?						
12. Do you enjoy going camping?						points
13. Do you like watching the news on TV?						
14. Do you enjoy reading?						
15. Are you good at doing exams?						points

Interview your partner (A) asking the questions **1-15** in the table below. Check the examples below, then write a score for your partner's answers on a scale of **0-4**.

Do you like/enjoy speaking English? Are you interested in speaking English?		Are you good at speaking English?	
-- Yes, I love/really like speaking English.	➡4 points	-- Yes, I'm really good at speaking English.	➡4 points
-- Yes, I like speaking English.	➡3 points	-- Yes, I'm pretty good at speaking English.	➡3 points
-- I don't mind speaking English. / It's OK.	➡2 points	-- I'm not bad at speaking English or I'm OK at speaking English.	
-- No, I don't (really) like speaking English.	➡1 point		➡2 points
-- No, I can't stand/hate speaking English.	➡0 points	-- No, I'm not very good at speaking English.	➡1 point
		-- No, I'm terrible/awful at speaking English.	➡0 points

Add the points for each section and write the total in the box. Check the results page(p.29) and read the information in the group that has the highest points total.

Question	RATE					TOTAL
	4	3	2	1	0	
1. Do you like karaoke?						
2. Are you good at drawing?						
3. Are you interested in fashion and design?						points
4. Do you like learning languages?						
5. Do you enjoy going to parties?						
6. Are you good at telling stories or jokes?						points
7. Do you like helping people?						
8. Are you good at remembering names?						
9. Do you enjoy going on family vacations?						points
10. Do you like playing sports?						
11. Do you enjoy going to watch live sports events?						
12. Are you interested in trying extreme sports?						points
13. Do you like doing research on the internet?						
14. Are you interested in learning new things?						
15. Are you good at puzzles and quizzes?						points

COMMUNICATE   Results

Group 1

Artist /
Craftsperson

You are a creative person. You are good at singing or playing musical instruments. You are imaginative and artistic. You also enjoy making things. You are fashionable and have your own individual style. You don't like following other people. You shouldn't work in an office. You are very independent and like spending time by yourself. You are a bit of a loner.

Suitable jobs: Artist, architect, chef, fashion designer, interior designer, musician

Group 2

Performer /
Entertainer

You are an entertainer or joker. You like performing in front of other people. You are good at telling stories. You are a cheerful, friendly person and love having fun. You enjoy being in large groups. You don't like being on your own at home. You prefer going out and partying. You are a city person and enjoy living in lively places.

Suitable jobs: Actor, comedian, journalist, politician, salesperson, teacher, TV presenter

Group 3

Helper / Carer

You like helping other people and are very caring, polite and honest. You can be a little shy and reserved, and don't like being the center of attention. You are cheerful and good at motivating people. You are family-minded and you are interested in doing volunteer work in your local community. You enjoy being at home with your family and also like eating out with friends.

Suitable jobs: Care worker, flight attendant, homemaker, NGO/volunteer worker, nurse, secretary/personal assistant

Group 4

Adventurer /
Doer

You are very outgoing. You are good at sports and enjoy doing physical things. You are very hardworking and energetic. You are very reliable and are loyal to your friends. You don't like sitting at home being lazy. You prefer going out and exercising. You are competitive and enjoy competing against others.

Suitable jobs: Businessperson, construction worker, doctor, emergency worker, lawyer, member of the armed forces, P. E. teacher, police officer

Group 5

Thinker /
Philosopher

You love reading and searching the internet. You are intelligent and like spending time at home. You enjoy watching movies and TV dramas, especially mysteries and crime dramas. When you are with friends, you like talking about news events or culture but don't like gossiping. You are not loud or outgoing, and you enjoy being by yourself.

Suitable jobs: Librarian, researcher, scientist, student, teacher

READ   Star Signs

A Complete the table below with information about yourself. When you have done this, interview two partners and write their answers in the space provided.

1. How would you describe your personality? (Positive)
2. How would you describe your personality? (Negative)
3. What do you like doing in your free time?
4. When is your birthday?
5. What is your star sign?

	YOU	SCORE※
1.		
2.		
3.		
4.		
5.		

	Partner 1	SCORE※
1.		
2.		
3.		
4.		
5.		

	Partner 2	SCORE※
1.		
2.		
3.		
4.		
5.		

※See the next page in details.

DL 11 · CD 11

B Read about your star sign below. How accurate do you think it is? Write a mark out of 10 for how similar it it to your personality on the previous page.

(10 = 100% exactly the same as you are ⇔ 0 = totally different to your personality)

Star sign	Personality & interests
Capricorn The Goat Dec. 23 - Jan. 20	Capricorns are shy and reserved. They are very practical and hardworking. They are loyal to their friends and family, but can be pessimistic and too sensitive. They like hobbies that can be done at home. They are good at cooking, painting and doing crafts. They don't like partying or going out to crowded places.
Aquarius The Water Carrier Jan. 21 - Feb. 19	Aquarians are very honest and intelligent. They are independent, easygoing and like to go their own way. They are sometimes thought to be cold and can be loners. They love technology and are really into computers and video games. They have a lot of different kinds of interests and enjoy socializing and volunteering.
Pisces The Fish Feb. 20 - Mar. 20	Pisces are kind, emotional and romantic people. They are imaginative and fun-loving. However, they can be nervous and sometimes give up too easily. They love all water related sports and activities. They enjoy fishing and hanging out at the beach with friends. They also love dancing and watching movies.
Aries The Ram Mar. 21 - Apr. 20	Aries are energetic and active. They are warm and generous. Sometimes, they can be too competitive and a little wild. They get bored easily and find it hard to relax. They really love playing sports, listening to loud music and watching action movies. Aries like getting attention, so they love performing, such as singing karaoke.
Taurus The Bull Apr. 21 - May 21	People with the star sign Taurus are relaxed and patient. Luxury, comfort and pleasure are important to them. They are sometimes a little stubborn and lazy. They love chilling out and enjoy relaxing at home by themselves or with friends. They love to eat and go shopping. Being artistic, they are into the arts and like music.
Gemini The Twins May 22 - Jun. 21	Geminis are smart. They like to know everything and everyone. They also like to do everything quickly. They are very sociable but can sometimes seem childish. Travel is popular for Geminis. They also love partying and being sociable. Geminis are good at communicating and love gossiping. They enjoy posting on social media.
Cancer The Crab Jun. 22 - Jul. 21	Cancers are charming and attractive. They are very loyal friends and are also very caring. They are passionate and creative, but can be moody and are easily hurt. They enjoy relaxing in a hot bath and daydreaming. They love beautiful things and like to look good and make their homes look good. They are good at making friends.
Leo The Lion Jul. 22 - Aug. 21	Leos are confident and outgoing. They are entertainers and love being the center of attention. They are natural leaders but sometimes can be arrogant and bossy. They like looking good, and their hair is very important. They enjoy performing, especially dancing and playing music. They love telling jokes, and meeting new people.
Virgo The Virgin Aug. 22 - Sep. 23	Virgos are hard workers who are very helpful. They are very organized and plan everything. They are perfectionists, and this can make them too critical. They prefer intellectual activities to physical ones. They love studying and learning new skills. Education is important to them. They also like helping other people.
Libra The Scales Sep. 24 - Oct. 23	Librans are good listeners and are sociable. They hate to be alone. They are thoughtful and interested in the world around them, but can be uncertain and think too much. They love hanging out with friends, going on dates or watching movies. They also love DIY and tidiness. They hate mess and can't stand arguments.
Scorpio The Scorpion Oct. 24 - Nov. 23	Scorpios are strong and independent and don't like doing things in large groups. They are passionate but can be quiet, shy and reserved. They are ambitious about their careers and are workaholics. They are good at individual sports, such as martial arts. They also enjoy doing yoga to relax.
Sagittarius The Archer Nov. 24 - Dec. 23	Sagittarians are warm, cheerful and energetic. They are optimistic and fun-loving. They are very honest, but are sometimes rude. They can be wild and unpredictable. They love all animals and nature. They enjoy traveling and camping. They are good at playing sports, especially team sports. They like being surrounded by friends.

WRITE

What are you like?

A Complete this student's description about his personality, likes, dislikes and abilities. Use the words from the vocabulary box below to help you.

> I am a friendly and _____ person. I like meeting my
> _____ and going shopping with them. I also like meeting new people.
> In addition, I'm _____ and organized. For example, I always do
> my _____ and I'm never late for _____ . I also consider
> myself to be artistic and _____ . I like drawing and
> _____ . I also like writing science _____ stories.
> However, I'm a little impatient. I don't like _____ for things. I don't like it
> when my friends are _____ , for example. I can also be stubborn at times.
> I like to do things my way. And finally, my younger sister thinks that I'm sometimes
> _____ . But that's just because I'm trying to help her with her studies.

> fiction   class   painting   homework   hardworking
> bossy   sociable   waiting   friends   late   imaginative

B Describe your likes, dislikes, abilities and personality. Circle three or four words from the list below that describe your personality:

> creative   imaginative   artistic   cheerful   friendly   caring   polite   honest
> cheerful   family-minded   outgoing   hardworking   reliable   loyal   patient
> confident   organized   energetic   competitive   intelligent   quiet   loud   romantic

C Complete the chart below with examples of your likes, dislikes, abilities, and personality.

LIKES	DISLIKES
GOOD AT	**NOT GOOD AT**
PERSONALITY (Positive)	**PERSONALITY (Negative)**

D Write about your likes, dislikes, abilities and personality using the examples and details from **B** and **C**.

What are you like?

VOCABULARY

DL 12   CD 12

Adjectives		easygoing *B1*	moody *B2*	sensitive *B2*
active *B1*		emotional *B1*	nervous *A2*	shy *A1*
ambitious *B1*		energetic *A2*	optimistic *B2*	sociable *B2*
arrogant *B2*		generous *B1*	organized *A2*	stubborn *B1*
artistic *B1*		hardworking *	outgoing *	thoughtful *B2*
bossy *B2*		honest *B1*	passionate *B2*	uncertain *B1*
calm *B1*		imaginative *	patient *B1*	unique *B1*
caring *B2*		impatient *A2*	pessimistic *B2*	unpredictable *B1*
charming *B2*		independent *B1*	practical *B1*	wild *A2*
cheerful *B1*		intelligent *A2*	quiet *A1*	worried *A2*
competitive *B1*		irresponsible *B2*	relaxed *A2*	**Noun**
confident *A2*		jealous *B1*	reserved *B1*	perfectionist *
creative *A2*		loud *B1*	reliable *B1*	**Verbs**
curious *B1*		loyal *B1*	romantic *A2*	preter *A2*

A Match each definition with the words on the right.

1. Someone who refuses to change their attitude: _____
2. Likely to change quickly and without reason: _____
3. A person who has very high standards and wants everything to be correct: _____
4. Someone who believes good things will happen: _____

    a. unpredictable
    b. perfectionist
    c. stubborn
    d. optimistic

B Complete the list below by adding negative prefixes to make opposites of the words listed on the left.

predictable	↔	*unpredictable*
organized	↔	
responsible	↔	
patient	↔	
honest	↔	
reliable	↔	

C Choose words from the box that best complete the questions. Answer the questions.

> worried   ambitious   romantic   prefer   artistic

1. Would you describe yourself as [_____]?   A: _____

2. Do you [_____] reserved or outgoing people?   A: _____

3. Are you [_____]? Are you good at drawing?   A: _____

4. Are you an [_____] person?   A: _____

5. Do you get [_____] easily or are you easygoing?   A: _____

D *Crossword:* Complete the crossword using the hints below.

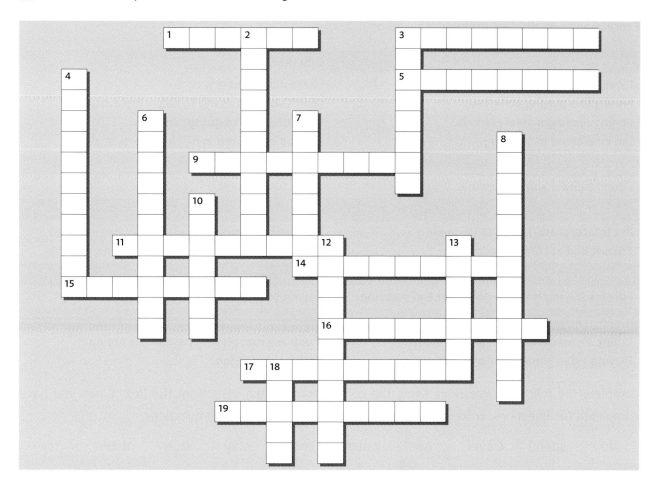

Across

1.

3. He is really _____ .
   He never admits he is
   wrong.

5.

9. I will fix it for you. I'm
   quite _____ and
   good with my hands.

11.

14. I'm going to get a high
    score in the test.
    I'm _____ I'll pass.

15. 　16.

17. They are extremely _____ . They want to
    become the No.1 band in the world.

19. He always cries when he watches _____
    scenes in movies and dramas.

Down

2. 　3.

6. My sister is so _____ .
   She does everything by
   herself.

4.

8. She's such a _____
   _____ . She notices
   every little mistake.

7.

10. I'm always _____ before exams. They
    make me stressed.

12.　13. I'm so _____ of
    you. I wish I was going
    to California with you.

18. Teenagers can be very _____ . Happy one
    minute and angry the next.

LANGUAGE REVIEW

Expressing likes, dislikes, preferences, and opinions.

LIKES	DISLIKES
I **love** watching American dramas on TV.	I **hate** doing laundry.
I **really like** playing volleyball.	I **can't stand** listening to heavy metal music.
I **enjoy** reading mystery novels.	I **don't really like** going camping.
I'm **interested in** traveling.	I'm **not interested in** playing sports at all.

Neutral	
I **don't mind** doing housework.	

Abilities	
I'm **(quite/pretty) good at** swimming.	I'm **terrible at** singing.
I'm **not bad at** playing badminton.	I'm **not very good at** dancing. I have no rhythm.

Preferences	
I **prefer** staying home **to** going out and partying.	I'm not so **crazy about** shopping.

Opinions	
I **think** snowboarding is really exciting.	**If you ask me,** playing pachinko is boring.
Playing video games is interesting.	I'm **afraid of** flying.

Complete the following questions using the correct form of the verb from the box. When you have completed the questions, write your answers. Then, ask your partner the questions.

do	spend	travel	go	watch	cook	play	study	listen	try

1. Do you enjoy _____ to see live concerts?

A: _____

2. Are you interested in _____ abroad in the future?

A: _____

3. Do you prefer _____ movies or TV dramas?

A: _____

4. Do you think _____ video games is interesting?

A: _____

5. What housework don't you mind _____ ?

A: _____

6. What subjects didn't you like _____ at high school?

A: _____

7. What kind of music do you hate _____ to?

A: _____

8. What kind of food are you good at _____ ?

A: _____

9. What sports are you afraid of _____ ?

A: _____

10. How do you like _____ your free time?

A: _____

Write a score (1-5)* in the boxes below to show how well you can do each part of the module. If you can't do any part well, go back to the page and practice again.

* 1 : Not at all   **2 :** A little   **3 :** OK   **4 :** Well   **5 :** Very well

UNIT 3

SCAN

I can scan for information about people's personalities (p.23). ·····

FOCUS

I can ask and answer questions about likes, dislikes, abilities and personalities (p.24). ····

LISTEN

I can understand a job interview for a flight attendant (p.25-26). ·····

COMMUNICATE

I can answer detailed questions about likes and abilities (p.27-29). ·····

UNIT 4

READ

I can read and understand information about star signs (p.30-31). ·····

WRITE

I can write about my likes, dislikes, abilities and personality (p.32-33). ·····

VOCABULARY

I can understand vocabulary related to personalities (p.34-35). ·····

PROJECT A

What do you know about your classmates?

First, write the correct questions below. Then ask 10 classmates and mark their answers in the tables below.

1. How many classmates are NOT from Kanto prefecture?

Q *Are you from Kanto? or Where are you from?*

From Kanto(Number)	Not from Kanto(Number)	From Kanto(%)	Not from Kanto(%)

2. How many classmates belonged to a sports club in high school?

Q

Belonged to a sports club(Number)	Didn't belong to a sports club (Number)	Belonged to a sports club (%)	Didn't belong to a sports club (%)

3. How many classmates have a part-time job at a restaurant?

Q

In a restaurant (Number)	Not in a restaurant (Number)	No part-time job (Number)	In a restaurant (%)	Not in a restaurant (%)	No part-time job (%)

4. How many classmates belong to a club at university?

Q

Belong to a club (Number)	Don't belong to a club (Number)	Belong to a club (%)	Don't belong to a club (%)

5. How many classmates want to study abroad in the future?

Q

Want to study abroad (Number)	Don't want to study abroad (Number)	Want to study abroad (%)	Don't want to study abroad (%)

6. How many classmates want to work in Tokyo after they graduate?

Q

Want to work in Tokyo (Number)	Don't want to work in Tokyo (Number)	Want to work in Tokyo (%)	Don't want to work in Tokyo (%)

RESULTS

Draw a pie chart showing your data from the previous page.

1. How many classmates are NOT from Kanto prefecture?

4. How many classmates belong to a club at university?

2. How many classmates belonged to a sports club in high school?

5. How many classmates want to study abroad in the future?

3. How many classmates have a part-time job at a restaurant?

6. How many classmates want to work in Tokyo after they graduate?

REPORT

Write the results of your survey.

All but two students in my group are from Kanto. Six students have a part-time job at a restaurant, but three students don't work part time.

PRESENTATION

Take turns explaining the results of your survey to your classmates using the pie charts from the previous page.

PROJECT B

What jobs match your classmates' personalities?

Ask 5 students about their personality. Then, note their answers (**A, B, C, D, E**) and their scores (**1, 2, 3, 4, 5**) in the tables below.

Answer	A: Strongly agree	B: Agree	C: It depends	D: Disagree	E: Strongly disagree
Score	5	4	3	2	1

1. You are artistic and creative.

	Student 1	Student 2	Student 3	Student 4	Student 5
Answer					
Score					

2. You are hardworking and organized.

	Student 1	Student 2	Student 3	Student 4	Student 5
Answer					
Score					

3. You are sociable and outgoing.

	Student 1	Student 2	Student 3	Student 4	Student 5
Answer					
Score					

4. You are shy and reserved.

	Student 1	Student 2	Student 3	Student 4	Student 5
Answer					
Score					

5. You are intelligent and thoughtful.

	Student 1	Student 2	Student 3	Student 4	Student 5
Answer					
Score					

6. You are energetic and sporty.

	Student 1	Student 2	Student 3	Student 4	Student 5
Answer					
Score					

RESULTS

Draw spider charts showing your data from the previous page.

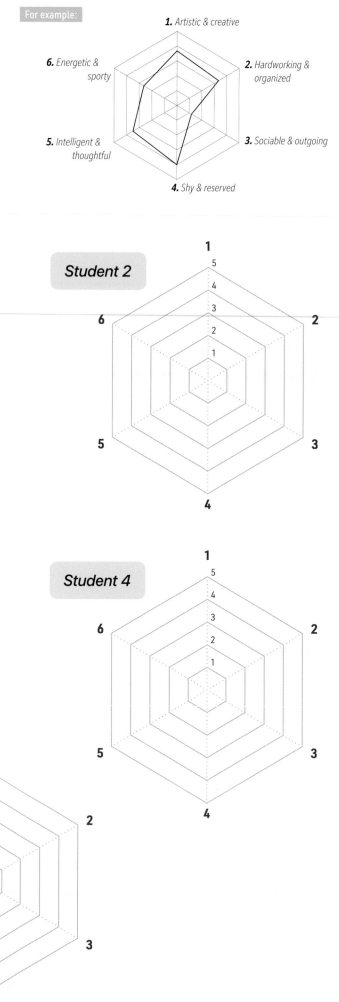

For example:

1. Artistic & creative
2. Hardworking & organized
3. Sociable & outgoing
4. Shy & reserved
5. Intelligent & thoughtful
6. Energetic & sporty

Student 1

Student 2

Student 3

Student 4

Student 5

REPORT

Write the results of your survey. Look at the Communicate results (p.29) which matches likes, dislikes, abilities, and personalities with jobs. Decide which jobs best match your classmates.

For example: *Student 1 is very artistic and creative. I think he should become a fashion designer because he likes clothes.*

PRESENTATION

Take turns explaining the results of your survey to your classmates using the spider charts from the previous page.

MODULE 3

Recommendations

GOALS:

 Can you scan for information about famous places in Japan?

 Can you recommend places to visit in Japan?

 Can you understand recommendations for places to visit in Kyushu?

 Can you answer general knowledge questions about Japan?

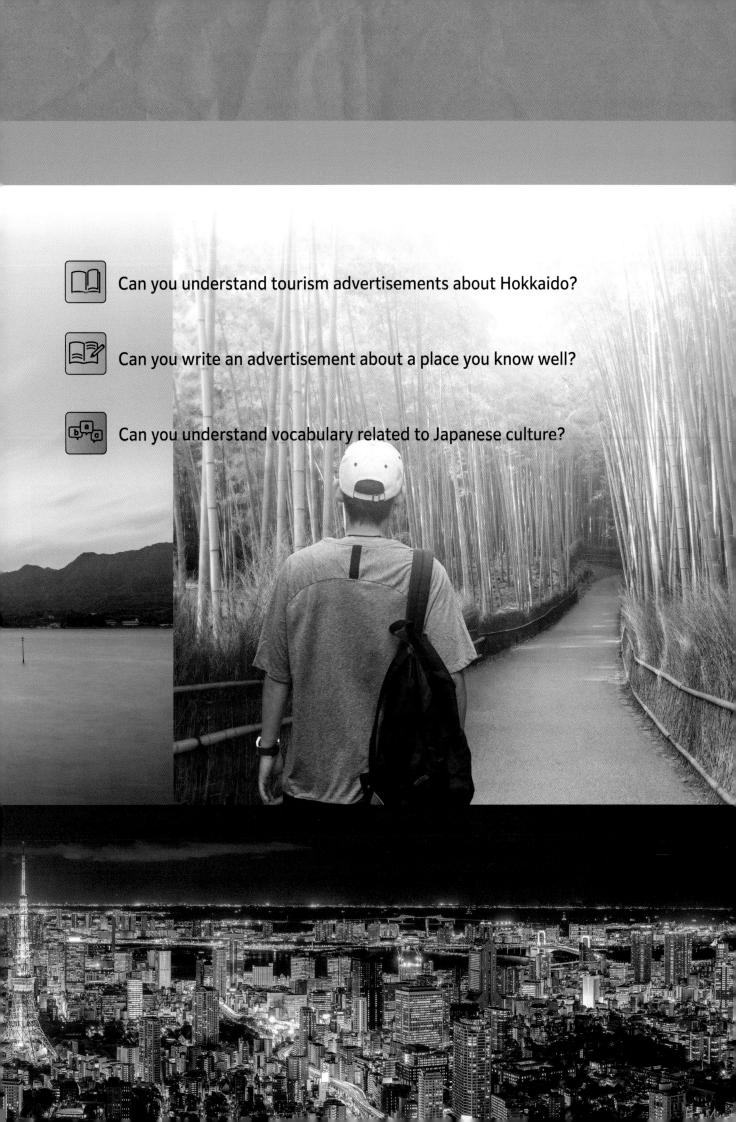

Can you understand tourism advertisements about Hokkaido?

Can you write an advertisement about a place you know well?

Can you understand vocabulary related to Japanese culture?

MATCH

Look at pictures **1** - **6**. Try to guess which place or event matches each prefecture **a** - **f**. Write the letter of the prefecture in the space next to the pictures below. Then, write the name of the prefecture in the space under each mascot and map.

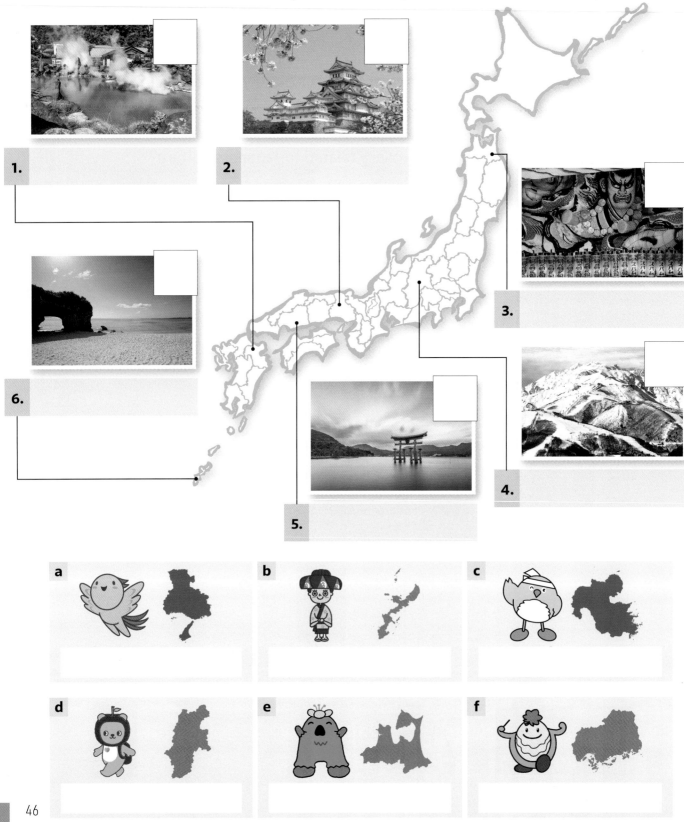

1.

2.

3.

4.

5.

6.

a

b

c

d

e

f

SCAN

Making plans and giving recommendations

A *Scanning for information:* <u>In 4 minutes</u>, scan the texts below to find the key information. Check your answers on the previous page.

B Read the texts again and write the name of the sightseeing places or events under pictures **1-6** on the previous page.

🎧 DL 13   ⊙ CD 13

1.
This is one of the most well-known hot spring resorts in Japan and it is my favorite place in Kyushu. The natural hot baths are so relaxing and refreshing. The town is really interesting too. There are also lots of different hell pools or jigoku. The "Blood Pond Hell" is the most impressive. The water is bright red. If you like hot springs, I recommend visiting Beppu in Oita prefecture.

2.
There are summer festivals held in various parts of Aomori prefecture. The largest festival is the Nebuta Matsuri in Aomori city. The parades have huge, colorful floats and traditional singing and dancing. It is a lot of fun and everyone wears traditional Haneto costumes. The food is delicious too. There are lots of places selling fresh seafood. In my opinion, it is the most exciting festival in Japan.

3.
With awesome ski resorts and breathtaking natural beauty, Nagano prefecture is an ideal place for skiing and snowboarding. The 1998 Winter Olympics took place in Hakuba in Nagano. Hakuba has some of the highest snowfall in Japan. It is a traditional town with excellent local food and lively nightlife. You must go!

4.
Miyako Island is in the southernmost part of Japan, Okinawa prefecture. It has beautiful white sandy beaches, clear, blue water and coral reefs that are perfect for snorkeling and diving. The climate is mild and comfortable. Goya chanpuru is the most famous local dish. If you are into marine sports or like relaxing on a beach, this is definitely the place for you.

5.
Himeji Castle is one of Japan's 12 original castles and one of the most historic places in Japan. Many people think Himeji Castle is the most beautiful in Japan. It is also a very popular cherry blossom viewing spot in spring and can be very crowded in the Golden Week holiday period. If you can avoid busy days, a trip to this stunning castle in Hyogo prefecture will be an unforgettable experience.

6.
For anyone interested in traditional Japanese culture, Itsukushima Shrine is not to be missed. It is one of two UNESCO World Heritage Sites in Hiroshima prefecture and the views of the floating torii gate are spectacular. Wild deer walk freely around Miyajima Island and a cable car takes you to the top of Mt. Misen. It is one of the most scenic places in Japan!

C In pairs, discuss which of the famous sightseeing places you would most like to visit and give your recommendations for other places to visit in Japan.

FOCUS

A *Making plans:* Match phrases **1-6** with pictures **a-f** below.

1. I'm thinking of going surfing next weekend. · ☐

2. I'm planning to go to a fireworks festival in August. · ☐

3. I'd like to go camping this summer. · ☐

4. I want to go hiking on my day off. · ☐

5. I'm going shopping in Osaka next week. · ☐

6. I might go sightseeing in Tokyo during Golden Week. · ☐

a.  b.  c.

d.  e.  f.

B *Giving recommendations:* Match recommendations **7-12** with phrases **1-6** above.

7. If I were you, I'd go to Lake Biwa fireworks festival. It's awesome! · · · · · · · · · · · · · · · · · · · ☐

8. You should climb one of the local mountains. The views are beautiful. · · · · · · · · · · · · · · · · ☐

9. You must go to the night market in Dotonbori. You can buy great souvenirs there. · · · · · · · · ☐

10. Check out this camping website – it recommends lots of good camp sites. · · · · · · · · · · · · · ☐

11. You've got to see the Kaminarimon in Asakusa! · ☐

12. Why don't you go to Enoshima? I think it's the best place for surfing. · · · · · · · · · · · · · · · · · ☐

C 💬💬 *Let's talk:* (a) In pairs, one person should use phrases **1-6**. The other person should give recommendations using phrases **7-12**.

(b) In pairs, one person make plans to take trip somewhere in Japan. The other person then gives their own recommendations.

For example:

> *A: I'm planning to go to Kyoto next month.*
> *B: Really? If I were you, I'd visit Kinkaku-ji Temple. I think it's the most beautiful temple in Japan.*

LISTEN

Travel podcast

 DL 14   CD 14

A Listen to the first part of the travel podcast. Write the area's name in the box and put a check mark (✓) in the correct places located in the area.

Area name: _____

B Read the section of the podcast talking about food and try to guess the missing words. Then listen to the podcast again, check your answers and complete it below.

 DL 15   CD 15

Food

In my _____ , the food in Kyushu is some of the best in all of Japan.

I mentioned the restaurants in Fukuoka, and it is a really _____ place to eat

out. You have got to try Hakata ramen. It's the _____ of Fukuoka. And the

Mentaiko, which is cod roe (or cod eggs) that are often served spicy, is probably the

most _____ in Japan. I also really _____ trying the Motsunabe hot

pot with pork or beef offal. It is so delicious, especially when the weather gets cold.

Kumamoto prefecture is also _____ for its _____ food. The basashi

horse meat sashimi, and the tonkatsu fried pork cutlet are not to be _____ .

C Complete the details below about places to visit in Kyushu, recommended food, and what to do in spring and summer. Listen to the podcast again in order to check the information.

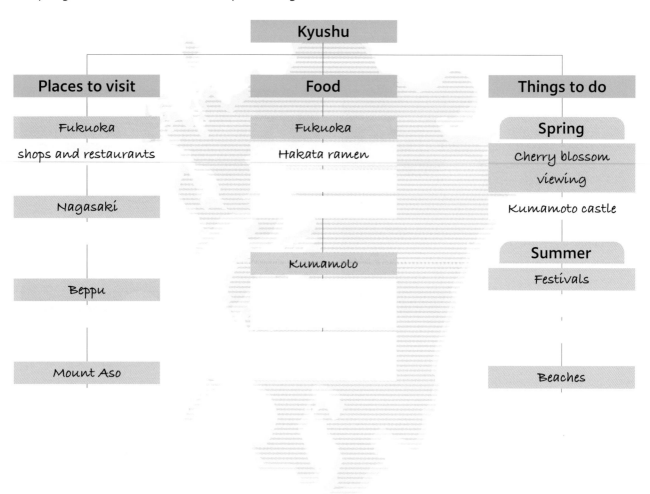

Kyushu		
Places to visit	**Food**	**Things to do**
Fukuoka	Fukuoka	Spring
shops and restaurants	Hakata ramen	Cherry blossom viewing
Nagasaki		Kumamoto castle
	Kumamoto	Summer
Beppu		Festivals
Mount Aso		Beaches

D 💬💬 Give your opinion!

1. Kyushu has the most beautiful nature in Japan.

Agree: _____ Disagree: _____

Why? _____

2. I think Kumamoto Castle is the most impressive castle in Japan.

Agree: _____ Disagree: _____

Why? _____

3. Summer is the best season in Japan. You can enjoy festivals and go to the beach.

Agree: _____ Disagree: _____

Why? _____

4. Would you like to visit Kyushu on vacation?

Yes: _____ No: _____

Where would you like to go? _____

Why? _____

COMMUNICATE

How well do you know Japan?

If you are into amusement parks, you should go to ...	Where is the best place to eat ramen noodles?	Name 3 World Heritage Sites in Japan.	**JAPANOPOLY RULES** In groups of three or four, use a pencil, and without looking, touch one of the dice in the box. Check the number, move that number of spaces and answer the question in that square.

JAPANOPOLY RULES

In groups of three or four, use a pencil, and without looking, touch one of the dice in the box. Check the number, move that number of spaces and answer the question in that square.

Name the 3 longest rivers in Japan.

What is the oldest university in Japan?

The best place to go sightseeing in Japan is ...

Where in Japan would you most like to live? Why?

Name 4 prefectures beginning with the letter "S".

I recommend going camping to ...

What is the largest fireworks festival in Japan?

JAPANOPOLY

What is the best month to visit Japan? Why?

Where is the best place to go skiing or snowboarding in Japan?

The best place for cherry blossom viewing (hanami) is ...

Name 4 rules in Japan that you think tourists should know.

What are the top three tourist attractions in Japan?

If you come to my hometown, you should try ...

In my opinion, the most impressive castle in Japan is ...

Finish

What was your best ever trip or vacation in Japan?

Lake Tazawa is the deepest lake in Japan. Where is it?

What is the second largest prefecture in Japan?

My favorite season in Japan is ...

Which area of Japan do you think has the most delicious food?

What souvenirs do you recommend buying from your home region?

Where is the best place to go surfing in Japan?

If you want to visit a temple or shrine in Japan, you should go to ...

Name the 5 biggest cities in Japan.

What is the second highest mountain in Japan?

If you like hot springs, I recommend going to ...

Did you go to the beach last year?

Name 4 interesting festivals in Japan.

↑ *Start*

READ

What do you know about Hokkaido?

A In pairs, discuss what you know about Hokkaido.

Example questions:

What famous places do you know? How is the weather? What food is Hokkaido famous for?

What recommendations can you give to tourists for things to do there?

B Read the phrases in **Part A** below (a-f). Then, try to complete the sentence. Next, read the phrases in **Part B** and complete the sentence by matching **Part A** with **Part B**.

The Best of Hokkaido

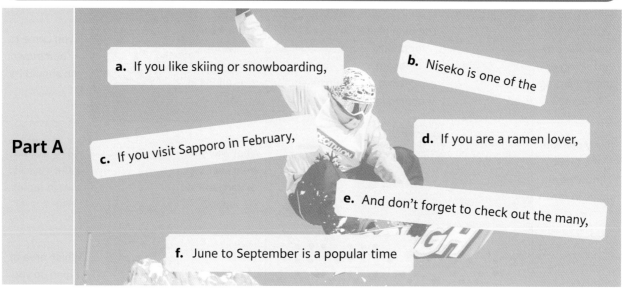

Part A

a. If you like skiing or snowboarding,

b. Niseko is one of the

c. If you visit Sapporo in February,

d. If you are a ramen lover,

e. And don't forget to check out the many,

f. June to September is a popular time

Part B

○ excellent shopping malls and restaurants in Sapporo.

○ you can see the impressive Snow Festival.

○ you'll love Niseko!

○ we recommend visiting the Ramen Village in Asahikawa.

○ most famous ski resorts in Japan.

○ to enjoy the nature.

DL 16   CD 16

C Read a tourism advertisement about Hokkaido, then complete the chart below.

The Best of Hokkaido

Incredible natural beauty as well as perfect snow conditions, if you like nature, skiing and snowboarding, you'll love Hokkaido! Niseko is one of the most famous ski resorts in Hokkaido. It is famous for its powder snow, which makes it a great place for winter sports. Also, the views of Mount Yotei are breathtaking. You should also visit Sapporo: the capital of Hokkaido. If you visit Sapporo in February, you can see the impressive snow festival. And don't forget to check out the many, excellent shopping malls and restaurants in Sapporo.

As for food, you have a wide choice. Treat yourself to Hokkaido's excellent seafood. If you have time, try visiting one of the many popular seafood markets. In addition, be sure to sample Hokkaido's other food specialty: ramen! If you are a ramen lover, we recommend visiting the Ramen Village in Asahikawa. It has a variety of dishes to choose from. Also, lamb barbecue is a local specialty that should not be missed.

Summer in Hokkaido is also fantastic. Hokkaido is cooler than other parts of Japan, which means it's ideal for camping. June to September is a popular time to enjoy the nature. You can try activities such as hiking and cycling. The weather at this time of year is great, so it's a perfect time to enjoy Hokkaido's incredible scenery.

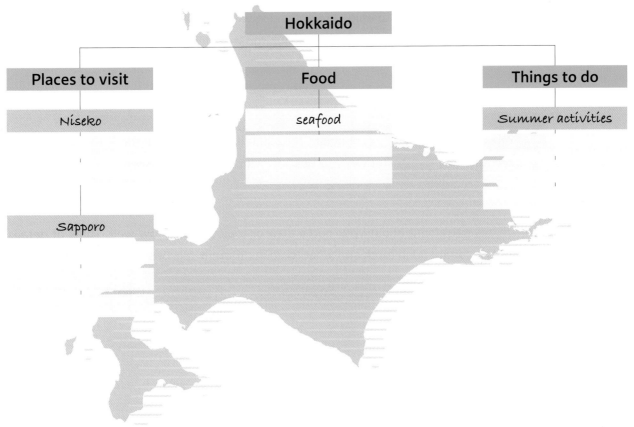

Hokkaido

Places to visit	Food	Things to do
Niseko	seafood	Summer activities
Sapporo		

A Complete this advertisement about Tokyo. Use the words from the vocabulary box below to help you.

The Best of Tokyo

There are so many incredible places to visit in Tokyo. If you like shopping, you'll _____ Ginza. All the famous fashion designer brands and department stores are there. Alternatively, younger people may prefer shopping in lively Harujuku. For _____, Tokyo has lots old and modern places to see. Asakusa is an older part of Tokyo with lots of traditional temples and it's very popular with tourists. And, if you have time, try visiting Meiji Jingu Shrine. It is one of the most _____ places in Tokyo. However, if you like modern places, be sure to check out Shinjuku – you'll love it!

For food, Tokyo has lots of amazing places to eat with different cuisines for everyone. Restaurants are everywhere and different areas specialize in different kinds of food. Shin-Okubo, for example, has the _____ Korean food in the capital . If you are a seafood lover, be sure to check out the fish at Tsukiji Outer Market, we _____ learning to make sushi.

Anytime is a good time to visit Tokyo. In spring, you should check out the _____ cherry blossoms in Ueno Park. It is also a great place to have a _____ picnic. You should also go to the top of the Skytree. The views are _____. In summer, going to a fireworks festival is also a a lot of fun. August is the time to enjoy fireworks festivals. Sumidagawa Fireworks Festival is one of the most _____ in Japan. But be careful, the weather at this time of year can be very hot and _____, so wear light clothes.

| relaxing | humid | popular | sightseeing | beautiful |
| breathtaking | historical | best | recommend | love |

B Think of a tourism advertisement about your home area or a place you know well. Think of details about places to visit, recommended food, and what to do in different seasons.

Places to visit	Food	What to do

C Write about your home area or a place you know well using the details from the previous page. Try to use phrases such as;

If you like … , you'll love… . You should/must …. You've got to …. I recommend …

A place you know well

VOCABULARY

DL 17　　CD 17

Adjectives

authentic C1 ....
awesome A2 ....
beautiful A1 ....
breathtaking B2 ....
colorful A2 ....
crowded A2 ....
excellent A2 ....
historic B1 ....
huge B1 ....
ideal A1 ....
impressive B2 ....
incredible B1 ....
interesting A1 ....

lively B1 ....
luxurious B2 ....
mild B1 ....
modern A2 ....
perfect A2 ....
refreshing + ...
relaxing B1 ....
scenic + ...
traditional B1 ....
unforgettable A2 ....
well-known A2 ....

Nouns

attraction B1 ....

building A2 ....
camping A2 ....
cherry blossom + ...
choice B1 ....
climate B1 ....
festival B1 ....
fireworks B1 ....
hiking A2 ....
hot spring + ...
museum A1 ....
nature A2 ....
nightlife B1 ....
plan A1 ....
resort B1 ....

season B1 ....
sightseeing A2 ....
souvenir B1 ....
specialty + ...
surfing A2 ....
tourist A2 ....
variety B1 ....

Verbs

check out + ...
eat out + ...
plan A2 ....
recommend B2 ....
(be) sure to + ...
take place + ...

A Match each definition with the words on the right.

1. No room to move: _____
2. Really big: _____
3. Has a beautiful view: _____
4. A famous place, person or thing: _____

a. well-known
b. scenic
c. huge
d. crowded

B Choose a word from the box and complete each sentence.

breathtaking	nightlife	museums	specialty

1. This restaurant is great. The beef is a _____.

2. Ueno Park in Tokyo is famous for its _____.

3. There are no restaurants or bars. The _____ is terrible.

4. The view from the top of this building is _____.

C Choose the words from the box that best complete the questions. Answer the questions.

season	recommend	luxurious	sightseeing	historic

1. Where is a good place to go for a [_____] vacation?　A: _____

2. Which festival do you [_____] going to?　A: _____

3. What prefecture is the best for [_____]?　A: _____

4. Are there any [_____] places to visit in your home area?　A: _____

5. What [_____] is the best time to visit Japan?　A: _____

56

D *Crossword:* Complete the crossword using the hints below.

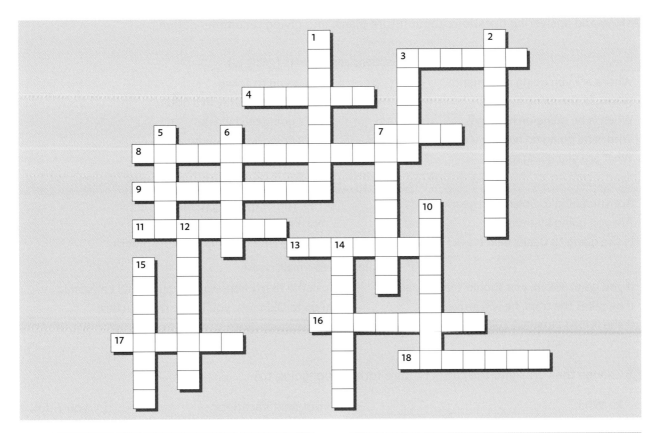

Across

3. Some parts of Tokyo are old and historic, but others are new and _____ .

4.

7.

8.

9.

11. Niseko's powder snow is _____ for snowboarding.

13. You should go to Hakodate, because the night view is _____ .

16.

17. I don't like quiet towns. I like big, _____ cities.

18.

Down

1. I love staying at five-star hotels, they are so _____ .

2. If you like _____ buildings, you'll love Kyoto.

3. The Louvre is the most famous _____ in Paris.

5. It is a difficult _____ whether to go to the beach or the mountains.

6.

7.

10. Osaka has lots of bars and restaurants. It's famous for its _____ .

12. If you are into Chinese food, I _____ Yokohama Chinatown.

14. The pizza at that restaurant is really _____ . It is the same as I ate in Italy.

15.

Asking and answering questions about future plans, and giving recommendations.

'Wh' questions and answers (going to)	
Where are you going next month?	I'm going to Tokyo.
Where is she going to stay?	She's going to stay in a hotel.
When is he going on holiday?	He's going next week.
Who is he going on holiday with?	He's going with friends.
What are you going to do?	I'm going shopping.

Yes/No questions (going to)	
Are you going to Spain next year?	Yes, I am. I'm going to Madrid.
Are you going by train?	No, I'm not. I'm going by bus.
Is she going to Osaka next week?	No, she isn't. She's going next month.

'If' + simple present + main clause	
If you go to Tokyo, you should see the palace.	If you come to my hometown, you should eat sushi.
If he takes the train, he will arrive early.	If you go to Okinawa, you'll love the beaches.
If she is into Japanese culture, she'll enjoy going to Kyoto.	

A Change the verbs into the correct future form using 'going to'.

1. What _____ in your next vacation?   [you / do]

2. When _____ to Osaka?   [you / go]

3. Who _____ in Kyushu?   [they / meet]

4. Where _____?   [he / eat]

5. I _____ authentic Chinese food.   [eat]

6. I _____ a fireworks festival next week.   [go]

7. They _____ at a traditional Japanese hotel.   [stay]

8. He _____ at a local restaurant.   [eat]

B Choose (Are /Is) and change the verbs into the future form using 'going to'.

1. _____ Okinawa?   [you / fly]

2. _____ any souvenirs?   [she / buy]

3. _____ to your hometown this summer?   [you / go]

4. _____ to Hokkaido?   [he / drive]

C Arrange the words in correct order.

1. nightlife / like / you / if / should / you / city / to / go / the

_____

2. culture / see / you / if / want / to / museum / you / go / a / should / to

_____

MODULE 3 SELF-CHECK

Write a score (1-5)* in the boxes below to show how well you can do each part of the module. If you can't do any part well, go back to the page and practice again.

* 1 : Not at all   **2 :** A little   **3 :** OK   **4 :** Well   **5 :** Very well

UNIT 6

📖 SCAN

I can scan for information about famous places in Japan (p.47). ································ ☐

🎧 FOCUS

I can recommend places to visit in Japan (p.48). ································ ☐

🔊 LISTEN

I can understand recommendations for places to visit in Kyushu (p.49-50). ············· ☐

👥 COMMUNICATE

I can answer general knowledge questions about Japan (p.51). ································ ☐

UNIT 7

📖 READ

I can understand tourism advertisements about Hokkaido (p.52-53). ················ ☐

📝 WRITE

I can write an advertisement about a place I know well (p.54-55). ················ ☐

🔤 VOCABULARY

I can understand vocabulary related to Japanese culture (p.56-57). ················ ☐

MODULE 4

Recipes

GOALS:

 Can you scan for information about recipes?

 Can you describe how to cook something?

 Can you understanding cooking instructions to make a pie?

 Can you describe Japanese food?

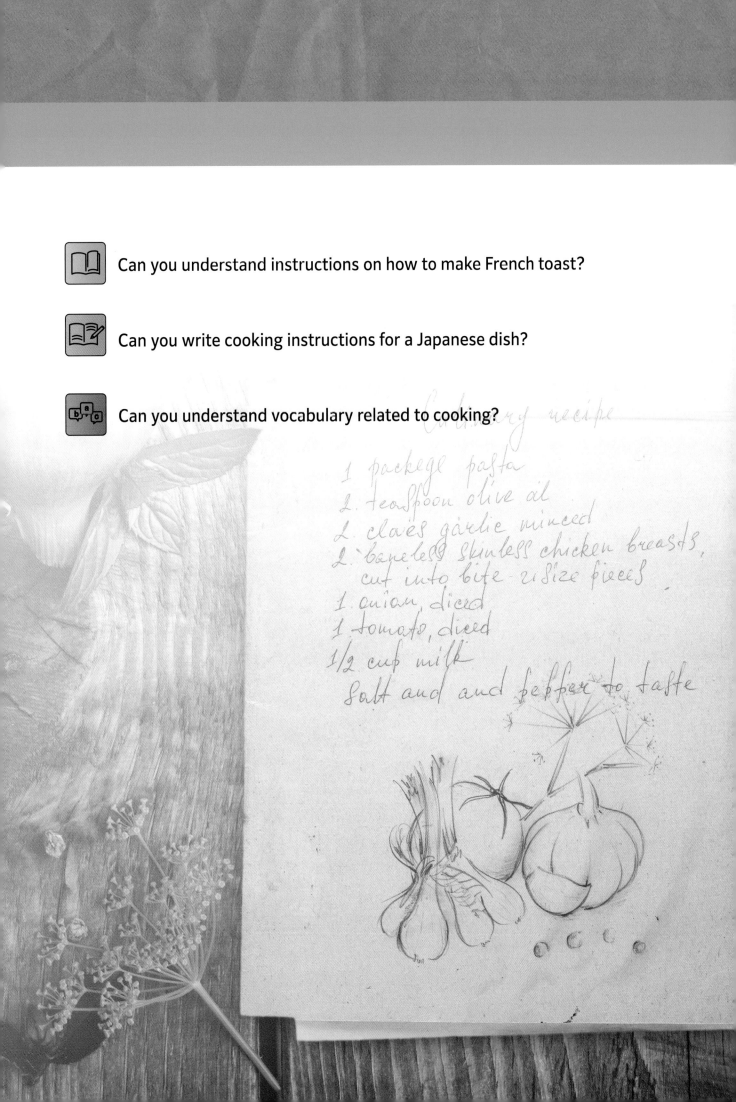

Can you understand instructions on how to make French toast?

Can you write cooking instructions for a Japanese dish?

Can you understand vocabulary related to cooking?

Culinary recipe

1. packege pasta
2. teaspoon olive oil
2. claves garlic minced
2. baneless skinless chicken breasts,
   cut into bite-size pieces
1. onion, diced
1. tomato, diced
1/2 cup milk
   Salt and and pepper to taste

MATCH

Look at pictures **a-i**. Try to guess the name of the dish and the ingredients needed to make it.

Next, arrange the pictures in the correct order to show how to make this dish.

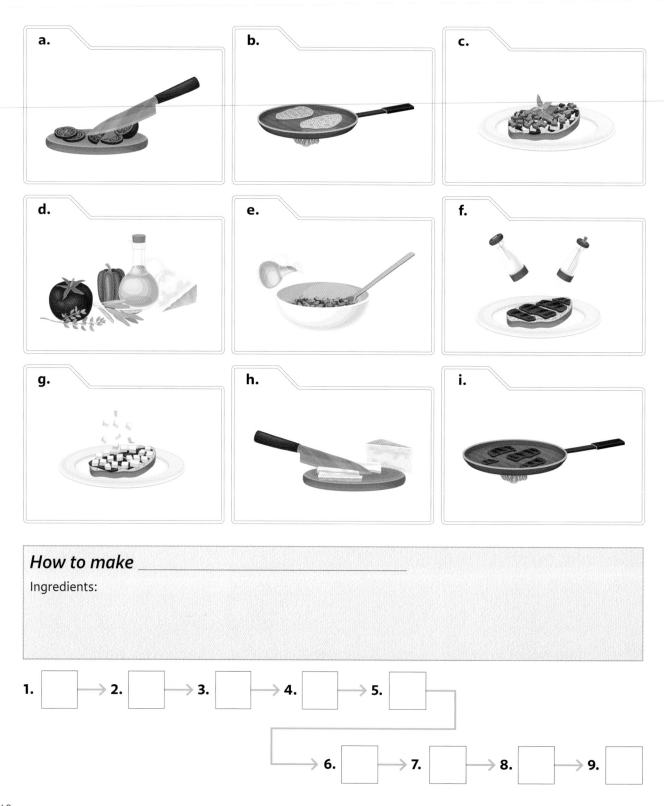

How to make _____

Ingredients:

1. ☐ → 2. ☐ → 3. ☐ → 4. ☐ → 5. ☐

6. ☐ → 7. ☐ → 8. ☐ → 9. ☐

SCAN

A *Scanning for information:* <u>In 4 minutes</u>, scan the texts below to find the key information. Check your answers on the previous page.

B Read the texts again to check name of the dish, the ingredients needed, and the order of the recipe you wrote on the previous page.

1.
This is an Italian starter called bruschetta. It is often eaten as a simple but delicious snack. The main ingredients you will need to make it are tomatoes, olive oil, and basil or other Mediterranean herbs. You can add red pepper, or other vegetables, if you like. Most importantly, you will also need crusty bread. People often use slightly old bread when making this snack. Today, we are going to add sliced ham, and diced Parmesan cheese but you don't need to add these ingredients if you would prefer a simple vegetarian snack.

2.
Before lightly toasting the bread in a frying pan with some olive oil, it is a good idea to rub the sliced bread with garlic for extra flavor.

3.
Next slice the tomatoes. You can use any kinds of tomatoes, but I recommend using plum tomatoes or cherry tomatoes as they have a richer flavor and are not too watery.

4.
After that, cut the Parmesan cheese into cubes. I think it works best if it is diced. Other Italian cheeses can be used. Mozzarella cheese is also very popular.

5.
Put the chopped tomatoes into a bowl together with any other vegetables and herbs you want to use. Then add some olive oil and mix these ingredients together.

6.
If you want to use meat, you can use raw ham or you can also lightly fry the meat in a frying pan.

7.
Place the meat on top of the toasted bread and add some salt and pepper for taste.

8.
If you want to add cheese, put the diced cheese on top of the slices of meat.

9.
Finally, add the mixed tomatoes, vegetables and herbs on top, and there you have it. It's a wonderfully tasty snack that you can prepare in minutes using any leftovers you have in the kitchen.

C In pairs, discuss what you are good at cooking and describe how you make it.

FOCUS

A Write the number of pictures **1-20** next to the matching cooking verbs below.

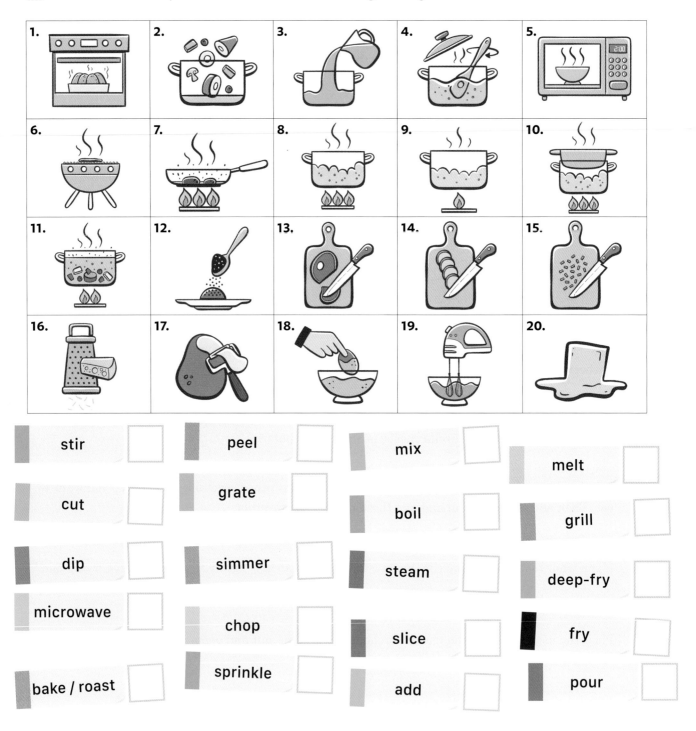

stir ☐	peel ☐	mix ☐	melt ☐
cut ☐	grate ☐	boil ☐	grill ☐
dip ☐	simmer ☐	steam ☐	deep-fry ☐
microwave ☐	chop ☐	slice ☐	fry ☐
bake / roast ☐	sprinkle ☐	add ☐	pour ☐

B With a partner, use the cooking verbs to describe how to cook something. Your partner will try and guess the dish you are describing.

For example:

Boil some rice and put it in a bowl. ***Add*** *a raw egg to the rice and* ***pour*** *a little soy sauce onto the egg.* ***Mix*** *the egg and rice together with your chopsticks.* ***Sprinkle*** *some furikake seasoning or dried seaweed on top.*

(Tamago kake gohan - Japanese-style egg rice)

LISTEN

Cooking class

 DL 19   CD 19

A Listen to a cooking class describing how to make a famous pie and describing its ingredients. Write the name of the dish in the box and put a check mark in the correct circles.

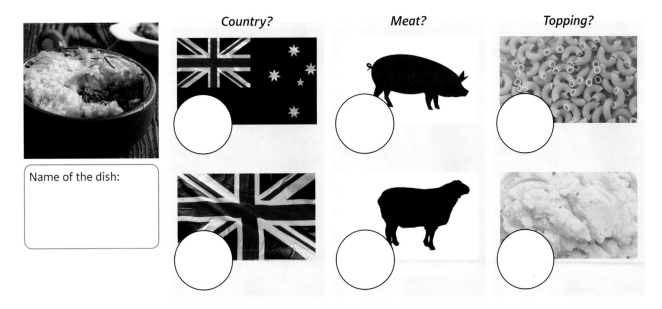

Country?   Meat?   Topping?

Name of the dish:

B Read the cooking instructions below and try to guess the missing words. Then listen to the instruction again, check your answers and complete the texts.

STEP 1   Preheat your oven to _____ ℃. Peel the potatoes, boil them, and then put them in a _____ . Mash them with a potato masher or a hand mixer. Next, peel the carrots and cut them. Chop the garlic and onion, and _____ the celery.

STEP 2   Heat the _____ in a frying pan for a few minutes then add the carrots, garlic, onion and celery. Next, add butter. Mix and fry everything for about 8 minutes. Then add _____ and pepper.

STEP 3   Add the _____ paste and mix for 2 minutes. Then add the flour and stir and _____ for an extra 3 minutes.

STEP 4   Slowly pour the meat and _____ into an oven dish. Next add the mashed potatoes on top of the dish. Spread the mashed potatoes with a _____ .

STEP 5   Place the dish into the oven and _____ for approximately 25 minutes until the top layer of mashed potatoes turns golden _____ . Now you can enjoy your Shepherd's pie!

C Listen to the instructions again. Complete the instructions on how to cook Shepherd's Pie below.

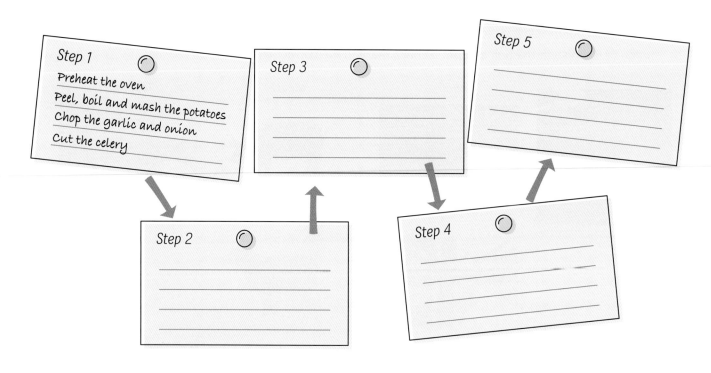

Step 1

Preheat the oven

Peel, boil and mash the potatoes

Chop the garlic and onion

Cut the celery

Step 3

Step 5

Step 2

Step 4

D 💬💬 Give your opinion!

1. I usually make my meals myself.

Agree: _____ Disagree: _____

Why? _____

2. I think natto is really tasty.

Agree: _____ Disagree: _____

Why? _____

3. I like eating meat more than fish.

Agree: _____ Disagree: _____

Why? _____

4. The food that I eat is pretty healthy.

Agree: _____ Disagree: _____

Why? _____

5. What dish are you best at cooking?

Answer: _____

COMMUNICATE

Describing Japanese food

A (Across clues)

You are "**A**", and have the across clues completed in the crossword. Your partner is "**B**" and has the down clues completed. Give hints for the Japanese food written in the across spaces. Do not say the name of the food or dish and also try not to speak Japanese. Try to give hints by explaining what kind of food it is, how it is made, what you eat it with, what color it is etc...

| For example: | 3 across ("*edamame*") |

-These are soybeans.
-They are boiled or steamed.
-They are often eaten as a side dish or snack.
-They are healthy and nutritious
-They are often salted and eaten with alcoholic drinks.

You are "**B**", and have the down clues completed in the crossword. Your partner is "**A**" and has the across clues completed. Give hints for the Japanese food written in the down spaces. Do not say the name of the food or dish and also try not to speak Japanese. Try to give hints by explaining what kind of food it is, how it is made, what you eat it with, what color it is etc...

For example: 1 down ("*tempura*")
-This is made with vegetables and seafood.
-The vegetables and seafood are dipped in a special batter.
-It is deep fried in very hot oil.
-My favorite are shrimp and renkon lotus root.
-It is eaten with special green tea salt or a dipping sauce made from fish stock, soy sauce and mirin.

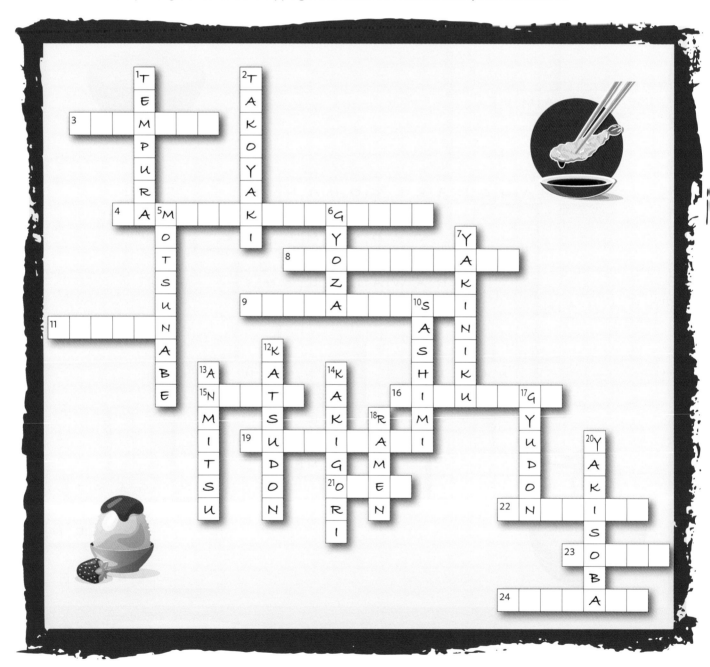

How to make French Toast

A French Toast is a popular breakfast dish that can be served with butter and syrup. Read the ingredients below. Try to guess the missing words.

Ingredients

- E_____
- Sliced b_____
- Sugar or s_____ (optional)

- M_____
- B_____

🎧 DL 20   💿 CD 20

B Read instructions **a–g** for cooking French Toast. Match them with the correct pictures below.

a. Put each slice of egg-covered bread into the frying pan. Gently stir and heat. Turn the bread over until each side is golden brown.

b. Break the eggs into a bowl and lightly beat them with a whisk or a fork.

c. Gently put a piece of sliced bread into the bowl. After a few seconds, turn it over so that the bread soaks.

d. Put a slice of butter into a frying pan. Use a low to medium heat and spread the butter around the pan.

e. Next pour milk into the bowl. You can add a little sugar or salt if you want. Then stir well.

f. Now serve your hot French toast. You can add toppings such as syrup, butter, or berries. Enjoy!

g. Get all the ingredients together. You will need butter, milk, sliced bread, and eggs. (Sugar and salt are optional).

C Put instructions **a–g** for cooking French Toast in the correct order.

1	2	3	4	5	6	7
g						

A Complete the description and the cooking instructions for Chicken Teriyaki below. Use words from the vocabulary box to help you.

Chicken Teriyaki

Description

Teriyaki Chicken is a _____ Japanese dish served with rice or _____ . It's very tasty and easy to _____ . It's made from chicken thigh with skin, and the teriyaki sauce has only four ingredients.

Ingredients

- Chicken thigh
- Cooking sake
- Mirin
- Soy sauce
- Sugar

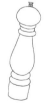

Cooking Instructions

Step 1: Pierce the chicken with a _____ . This will allow the teriyaki sauce to absorb into the chicken when cooking. Cut the chicken into _____ pieces.

Step 2: Heat a _____ pan and add oil. Make sure the skin is on the bottom side so that it cooks. _____ for about 5 minutes until the skin turns crispy brown. Then turn the chicken over and fry the other side.

Step 3: Add the cooking sake. _____ it over the chicken and let the chicken cook for a few minutes. Then add the mirin, followed by the soy sauce and then the sugar.

Step 4: Stir fry the chicken with the sauce until the chicken turns a _____ color.

Step 5: _____ the teriyaki chicken with rice, salad or vegetables and enjoy!

Fry	frying	fork	popular	make
salad	golden	Pour	Serve	smaller

70

B *Writing cooking instructions:* Think of a dish that you like. Describe the dish and its ingredients. Then write cooking instructions for the dish.

Name of the dish: _____

Ingredients:

Instructions:

VOCABULARY

Adjectives		Nouns		Verbs			
delicious A1		batter +		absorb B1		mix A2	
golden A2		bottom A1		add A1		rub B2	
low A2		flavor B1		bake A2		slice B2	
Mediterranean B1		flour A2		beat B1		peel B2	
medium B1		fork A2		break A1		place B1	
optional B2		garlic A2		chop B2		pour A2	
raw A2		ingredient(s) B1		cover A2		prepare A2	
tasty B1		layer B1		cut A1		roast A2	
vegetarian B1		lid A2		deep-fry +		serve A2	
Adverbs		mixture B2		dip B2		simmer +	
approximately B1		piece A1		follow A2		soak B2	
extra A2		sauce A2		fry B1		spread B2	
gently B2		skin B1		grill B1		sprinkle +	
		snack A2		microwave +		steam +	
		toast A2				stir B1	
						toast +	

A Match each definition with the words on the right.

1. A light meal: _____   **a.** flavor
2. The particular taste of something: _____   **b.** raw
3. Uncooked: _____   **c.** ingredients
4. The foods you use to make a dish: _____   **d.** snack

B Add a word that often goes with the adjective when talking about food.

- sliced   _bread_   • fried   _____
- grated   _____   • grilled   _____
- chopped   _____   • boiled   _____

C Circle a word that does not belong on the list.

Ingredients	flour	cheese	salt	bake
Vegetarian	vegetables	beans	ham	rice

D Choose the words from the box that best complete the questions. Answer the questions.

> vegetarian   delicious   flavor   snacks   sauce

1. What [_____] ice cream do you like best?   A: _____
2. What dessert do you think is [_____]?   A: _____
3. Do you often eat [_____] in the evening?   A: _____
4. Have you tried [_____] food?   A: _____
5. What is your favorite pasta [_____]?   A: _____

E *Crossword:* Complete the crossword using the hints below.

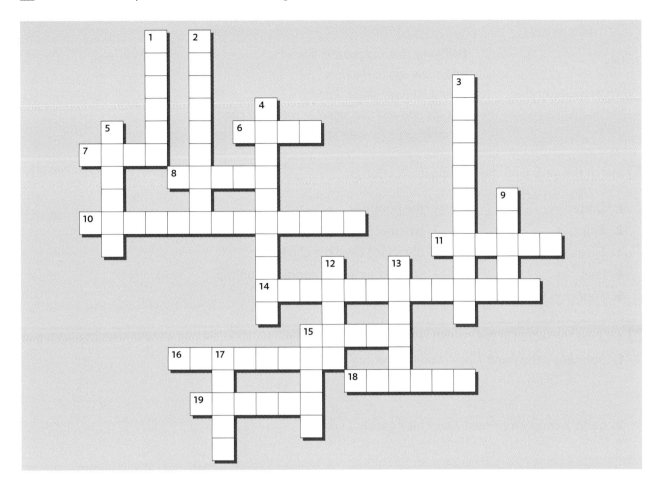

Across

6.

7.

8. I love pasta with carbonara _____ .

10. _____ food is delicious. I'm especially into French and Spanish cooking.

11. Cook on a _____ heat for 5 minutes.

14. Bake for _____ 10 minutes.

15.

16.

18. _____ some butter on the toast and serve.

19.

Down

1. My favorite _____ of ice cream is vanilla.

2. _____ the packet of rice for 2 minutes.

3. Mix all the _____ in a large bowl.

4. He doesn't eat meat. He's a _____ .

5. Toast the bread until it is _____ brown

9.

12.

13.

15.

17.

Sequencers	Imperatives
First,	**boil** some rice and put it in a bowl.
	add a raw egg to the rice.
Then, Next, After that,	**pour** a little soy sauce onto it.
	mix the egg and rice together with your chopsticks.
Finally,	**sprinkle** some furikake seasoning or dried seaweed on top.

A Match the verb with the cooking instructions.

1. Grate •   • the potatoes.

2. Boil •   • two pieces of bread.

3. Slice •   • the sauce over the chicken.

4. Peel •   • some cheese and sprinkle it on top.

5. Pour •   • the rice for 20 minutes.

B Arrange the words in the correct order.

1. potatoes / the / and / peel / boil / twenty / them / minutes / for

_____

2. garlic / chop / fry / next / and / it / gently / some

_____

C Choose the correct word and complete each sentence.

1. You have to _____ the garlic gently.	**a.** mix	**b.** fry	**c.** pour
2. Please _____ the food as soon as its ready.	**a.** serve	**b.** steam	**c.** prepare
3. We usually _____ the cake in an oven.	**a.** spread	**b.** beat	**c.** bake
4. Always _____ the frying pan with a lid.	**a.** chop	**b.** cook	**c.** cover
5. I usually _____ the eggs for three to four minutes.	**a.** rub	**b.** beat	**c.** break

D Choose the correct words from the box that best complete the sentences below.

deep-fry	approximately	layer	mix	simmer

1. First, _____ the ingredients together in a bowl.

2. _____ the sauce on a low heat.

3. Dip the vegetables in batter before you _____ them.

4. The meat takes _____ 30 minutes to cook.

5. For more taste, you can add an extra _____ of cheese.

MODULE 4 SELF-CHECK

Write a score (1-5)* in the boxes below to show how well you can do each part of the module. If you can't do any part well, go back to the page and practice again.

* 1 : Not at all   **2 :** A little   **3 :** OK   **4 :** Well   **5 :** Very well

UNIT 8

🔍 SCAN

I can scan for information about recipes (p.63). ⋯⋯⋯⋯⋯⋯⋯⋯⋯⋯⋯⋯⋯⋯⋯⋯⋯⋯⋯ ☐

🗣 FOCUS

I can describe how to cook something (p.64). ⋯⋯⋯⋯⋯⋯⋯⋯⋯⋯⋯⋯⋯⋯⋯⋯ ☐

👂 LISTEN

I can understand cooking instructions to make a pie (p.65-66). ⋯⋯⋯⋯⋯⋯ ☐

👥 COMMUNICATE

I can describe Japanese food (p.67-68). ⋯⋯⋯⋯⋯⋯⋯⋯⋯⋯⋯⋯⋯⋯⋯⋯⋯⋯⋯ ☐

UNIT 9

📖 READ

I can understand instructions on how to make French toast (p.69). ⋯⋯⋯⋯ ☐

✍ WRITE

I can write cooking instructions for a food dish (p.70-71). ⋯⋯⋯⋯⋯⋯⋯⋯ ☐

🔤 VOCABULARY

I can understand vocabulary related to cooking (p.72-73). ⋯⋯⋯⋯⋯⋯⋯⋯⋯ ☐

PROJECT C

What are Japan's best tourist attractions?

Think of two more questions about tourism in Japan and write them in boxes ④ and ⑤ below. Ask 10 students the questions in the table below about Japan. Make notes of the answers in the table below. Find out reasons for students' answers and also write them in the table below.

	① Which region in Japan do you think has the best local food? Why?	② Where is the best place for cherry blossom viewing in Japan? Why?	③ What is the most famous sightseeing spot in Japan? Why?	④	⑤
1					
2					
3					
4					
5					
6					
7					
8					
9					
10					

REPORT

Write about any similarities or differences in your results.

For example: *From my results, the best place for cherry blossom viewing in Japan is Kumamoto. Four students said the castle is amazing.*

PRESENTATION

Take turns explaining the results of your survey to your classmates and giving recommendations about tourist attractions in Japan.

For example: *You should visit Kumamoto prefecture because Kumamoto Castle is amazing.*

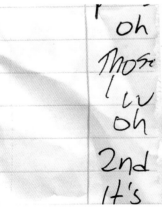

PROJECT D

Who enjoys cooking the most?

Choose 10 students and divide them into two groups of 5. Then, read out each statement below and note their answers (**A, B, C, D** or **E**) and scores (**5, 4, 3, 2, 1**) in the tables. Then write the total for each statement.

Answer	A: Strongly agree	B: Agree	C: It depends	D: Disagree	E: Strongly disagree
Score	5	4	3	2	1

1. I usually cook my own meals.

Group 1	Student 1	Student 2	Student 3	Student 4	Student 5	Total
Answer						
Score						/25
Group 2	Student 1	Student 2	Student 3	Student 4	Student 5	Total
Answer						
Score						/25

2. I am good at making desserts.

Group 1	Student 1	Student 2	Student 3	Student 4	Student 5	Total
Answer						
Score						/25
Group 2	Student 1	Student 2	Student 3	Student 4	Student 5	Total
Answer						
Score						/25

3. I often cook food from different parts of the world (international food).

Group 1	Student 1	Student 2	Student 3	Student 4	Student 5	Total
Answer						
Score						/25
Group 2	Student 1	Student 2	Student 3	Student 4	Student 5	Total
Answer						
Score						/25

4. I like to cook new recipes.

Group 1	Student 1	Student 2	Student 3	Student 4	Student 5	Total
Answer						
Score						/25
Group 2	Student 1	Student 2	Student 3	Student 4	Student 5	Total
Answer						
Score						/25

5. I enjoy cooking for other people.

Group 1	Student 1	Student 2	Student 3	Student 4	Student 5	Total
Answer						
Score						/25
Group 2	Student 1	Student 2	Student 3	Student 4	Student 5	Total
Answer						
Score						/25

RESULTS

Complete the charts below with the scores from the previous page.

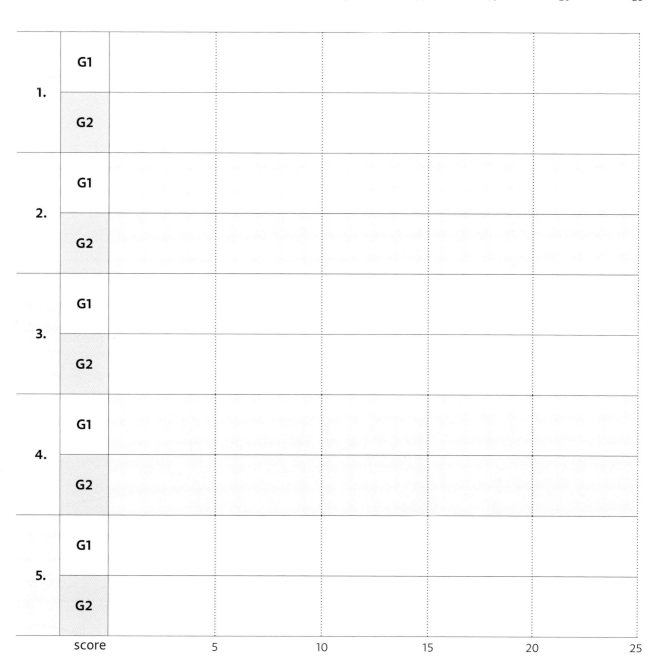

For example:

1. I usually cook my own meals.
2. I am good at making desserts.
3. I often cook food from different parts of the world.
4. I like to cook new recipes.
5. I enjoy cooking for other people.

REPORT

Write the results of your survey. Explain any differences between group 1 and group 2.

For example: *Group 1 likes cooking for other people more than group 2. For example, four students strongly agree but in group 2, only one student likes to cook for other people.*

PRESENTATION

Take turns explaining the results of your survey to your classmates using results from the previous page.

GOALS:

 Can you scan for information about modern devices?

 Can you describe how life in Japan has changed over time?

 Can you understand a lecture describing how life in Japan has changed over time?

 Can you read and answer statements about how the world has changed?

 Can you understand descriptions about life in the Edo period?

 Can you write about changes in society over time?

 Can you understand vocabulary related to change?

MATCH

Look at pictures **1-5**. Try to guess which old devices match modern devices **a-e** below. Write the letter in the space next to each number below.

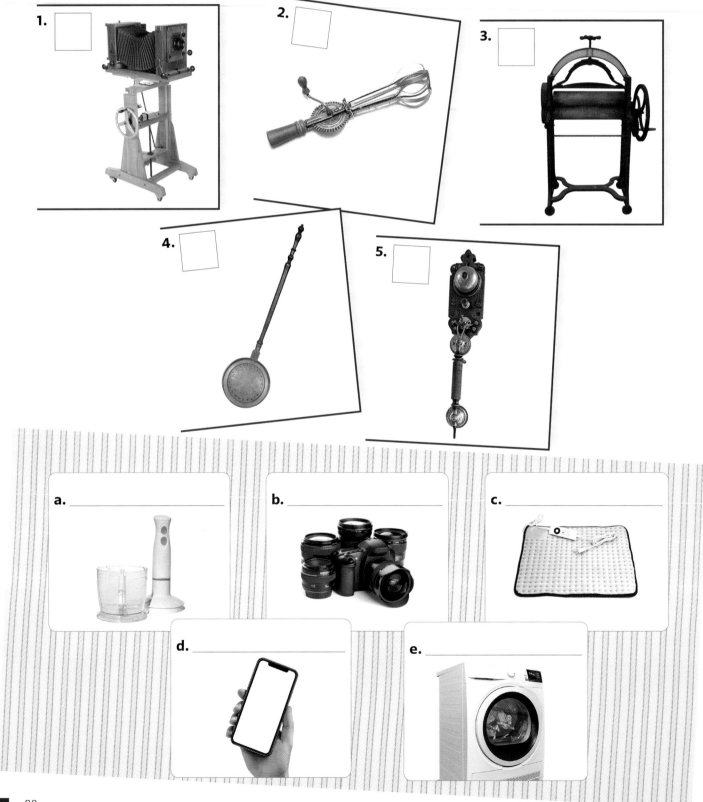

1.

2.

3.

4.

5.

a. _____

b. _____

c. _____

d. _____

e. _____

SCAN

A *Scanning for information:* In 4 minutes, scan the texts below to find the key information. Check your answers on the previous page.

B Read the texts again and write the name of the modern devices in the space above their pictures on the previous page.

🎧 DL 22   💿 CD 22

1.

This is an antique camera. Cameras used to be very big and couldn't be carried around easily. These days, people often take photographs and videos using their phones, however, people who are interested in photography prefer digital cameras that have different lenses for different kinds of shots.

2.

This is an old food mixer. Electric food mixers have only been around for about 100 years. In the past, cooks used to mix things with a spoon or a whisk. Then, in the late 1800s, the type of mixer in this picture was invented. This made it easier to mix things, so it wasn't as tiring as using an old whisk or spoon.

3.

Believe it or not, before we had washing machines and clothes dryers, people used this machine to dry clothes. It is called a mangle. You used to put wet clothes between the wooden rollers and turn the handle. The rollers would squeeze water out of the clothes, so they would dry quicker. Watch out for your fingers, though!

4.

These days, when the weather is cold, we can turn on an electric blanket to warm our bed before we go to sleep. Before electricity, people used to warm the bed with this device. You put hot coal in the metal bowl at the end and shut the metal lid. Then you warmed your sheets with the hot metal part. You had to be careful not to start a fire.

5.

Nowadays, smartphones are everywhere and we use them for everything. We can stream movies with them, download and listen to music, take photos and even, sometimes, people use them to make phone calls. In the past phones were very different and had to be attached to a phone line in the house. This old wooden phone was very big and used to hang on the wall.

C In pairs, discuss with your partner what you think have been the most important change in the last 100 years.

FOCUS

Describing how things have changed in Japan

A Match phrases **1-6** about Japan in the past with pictures **a-f**.

1. In Japan, eating meat was banned until the 19th century. · ☐

2. In the past, people used to travel by rickshaws. · ☐

3. Before TV and radio, people used to go to the theater for entertainment. · · · · · · · · · · · · · · ☐

4. During the Edo period, sumo was the most popular spectator sport. · · · · · · · · · · · · · · · · · · ☐

5. Soccer wasn't a popular sport in Japan a hundred years ago. · ☐

6. For hundreds of years people only wore traditional Japanese clothing. · · · · · · · · · · · · · · · · ☐

a.

b.

c.

d.

e.

f.

B Then, match phrases **1-6** with phrases **7-12** about Japan today.

7. Recently, people often use their smartphones for entertainment. · ☐

8. These days, people only use rickshaws for sightseeing. · ☐

9. Nowadays all kinds of meat dishes are very popular. · ☐

10. Now, a lot of people play and watch soccer. · ☐

11. And it is still popular today, though not as popular as in the past. · ☐

12. But kimonos are usually only worn on special occasions, these days. · · · · · · · · · · · · · · · · · · ☐

C 💬💬 *Let's talk:* In pairs, practice describing how life in Japan has changed over the years. Use the examples above to help you. Talk about things such as food, entertainment, transport, sport, and fashion.

For example: *In Japan, eating meat was banned until the 19th century. Nowadays, all kinds of meat dishes are popular. I still prefer eating fish and I love sushi.*

LISTEN

History lecture

🎧 DL 23   💿 CD 23

A Listen to the first part of a lecture explaining how transportation in Japan has changed over the years and put a check mark (✓) in the correct circles.

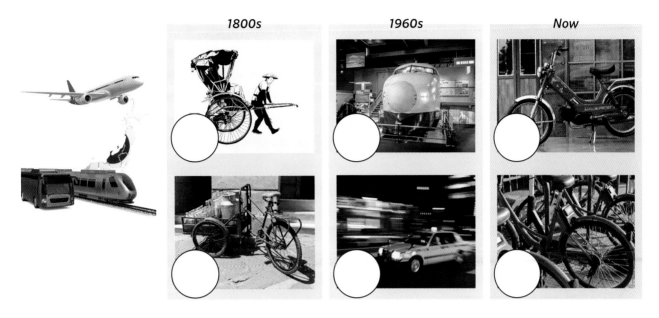

1800s   *1960s*   *Now*

🎧 DL 24   💿 CD 24

B Read the extracts from the lecture about sports and food below. Try to guess the missing words. Then listen again and check your answers.

> Sport has _____ a lot in Japan over the years. Two hundred years ago, people used to watch Japanese sports such as _____.
> During the 1980s and 90s, sports such as soccer, _____, and rugby became more popular. Nowadays, soccer is almost as popular as _____. However, many people still enjoy watching sumo on _____.

> Food has also changed a lot, but some things remain the _____.
> In the past, people used to eat a lot more fish, _____ wasn't as popular then. Also, people didn't eat Western-style _____ food a hundred years ago, but nowadays, it is very _____. For example, lots of people enjoy eating pizza and _____.

C Listen to the whole lecture. Based on the lecture, complete the diagram below to show how life in the past was similar or different to life today. Fill in the orange sections for transport, the blue sections for sport, the pink sections for food, and the green sections for entertainment.

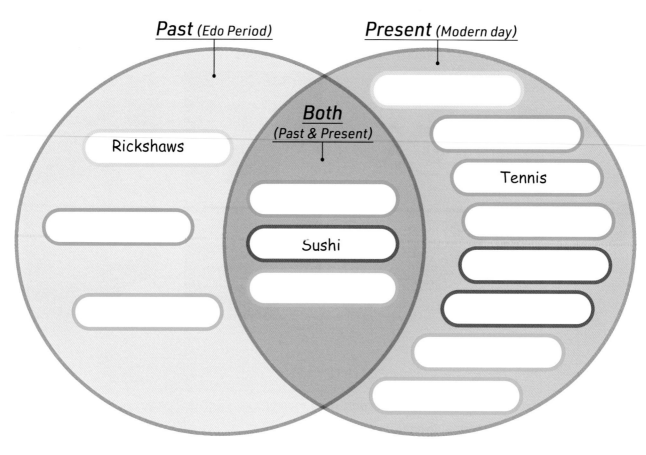

Past *(Edo Period)*   **Present** *(Modern day)*

Both
(Past & Present)

Rickshaws

Sushi

Tennis

D 💬💬 Give your opinion!

1. The food people eat today is not as healthy as in the past.

Agree: _____   Disagree: _____

Why? _____

2. Music and movies were better in the past than they are today.

Agree: _____   Disagree: _____

Why? _____

3. What forms of transport should we use to help protect the environment?

Forms of transport: _____

Why? _____

4. What sport do you think is the most popular in Japan?

Name of the sport: _____

Why? _____

COMMUNICATE How the world has changed! Partner A

Read statements **1-5** to your partner. Write your partner's guess in the answer column. Then, check the answers below. Give 1 point for each correct answer and write the total score in the box.

	Partner's answer	Points
1. Before rubber erasers were made, people in Europe used to erase pencil marks with _____. **a.** slices of cucumber **b.** boiled sweets **c.** old bread		
2. These days, runners often drink sports drinks during a marathon. In the past, runners in Europe would often have _____ during a race. **a.** bowls of minestrone soup **b.** small cups of espresso coffee **c.** alcoholic drinks, such as brandy or whisky		
3. Ancient Chinese people used _____ instead of toothbrushes. **a.** old pages from the daily newspaper **b.** chewsticks made from twigs of a willow tree **c.** special metal spoons designed to clean teeth		
4. Paintings on cave walls show prehistoric people shaving with _____. **a.** sharks teeth and clam shells **b.** special pieces of sandpaper **c.** small animals that looked like mice		
5. The Spartans punished cowards by _____. They believed this reduced their power for their journey to the Underworld. **a.** making them wear red lipstick **b.** shaving off their beards **c.** forcing them to wear yellow-colored clothes		

ANSWERS: 1. c 2. c 3. b 4. a 5. b   **TOTAL**

Evaluation

5 points	Amazing! You have a fantastic knowledge of history and understand what life was like in the past (or you are very good at guessing). Well done.
3-4 points	Very good! With a little more study you could become an excellent historian. It is important to know more about the past.
1-2 points	Not bad, but not so good either. If you discover more about the past, you may also understand more about things that may happen in the future.
0 points	No comment. You are clearly living in the present and are not interested in the past You also need to improve your guessing skills!

COMMUNICATE

How the world has changed!

Partner B

Read statements **1-5** to your partner. Write your partner's guess in the answer column. Check the answers below. Give 1 point for each correct answer and write the total score in the box.

	Partner's answer	Points
1. Before refrigerators were invented, in parts of Finland and Russia, people used to put _____ into milk to keep it from going bad. **a.** cheese **b.** brown frogs **c.** large rocks		
2. In England, until alarm clocks became popular, a "knocker-upper" was paid to wake people up in the morning. They used to _____ . **a.** light fireworks in the street every morning **b.** play the drums loudly until everyone woke up **c.** bang on people's bedroom windows with a long wooden stick		
3. In Roman times, people used _____ instead of toothpaste. **a.** a powder made from crushed bones and oyster shells **b.** a mixture of butter and raw eggs **c.** red wine mixed with sugar		
4. Instead of sleeping for six to eight hours each night, in the past people would sleep _____ . **a.** for 12 hours one night then not go to bed the next night **b.** for 2 hours in the middle of the night, 2 hours after lunch and 2 hours in the early evening **c.** for 4 hours, wake up for 1 or 2 hours to do chores and eat a light meal, then go back to sleep for another 4 hours		
5. The ancient Greeks considered the right side to be the lucky side. That's one reason why _____ . **a.** people drive on the right side of the road in Greece **b.** It is rude to shake hands with your left hand **c.** waving goodbye with your right hand is thought to be unlucky		

ANSWERS: 1. b 2. c 3. a 4. c 5. b   **TOTAL**

Evaluation

5 points	Amazing! You have a fantastic knowledge of history and understand what life was like in the past (or you are very good at guessing). Well done.
3-4 points	Very good! With a little more study you could become an excellent historian. It is important to know more about the past.
1-2 points	Not bad, but not so good either. If you discover more about the past, you may also understand more about things that may happen in the future.
0 points	No comment. You are clearly living in the present and are not interested in the past You also need to improve your guessing skills!

88

READ

A Look at the picture below. There are <u>10 items</u> that didn't exist in the Edo period. Circle the 10 things that weren't in the original picture.

LIFE IN EDO JAPAN

B Read the comments about the drawing showing life in Edo Japan on the previous page and check that you found the 10 mistakes.

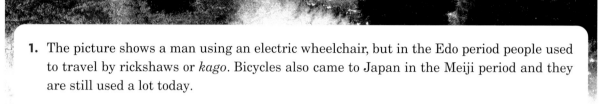

1. The picture shows a man using an electric wheelchair, but in the Edo period people used to travel by rickshaws or *kago*. Bicycles also came to Japan in the Meiji period and they are still used a lot today.

2. Portable stereo players, known as boomboxes, were popular in the 1980s, but didn't exist in the Edo period. Now, most people listen to music using their smartphones with wireless earphones or headphones, so they can listen to music wherever they are.

3. These days, stuffed toys are everywhere, especially those featuring a famous mouse. In Japan, American animation characters didn't become popular until the 1980s. In the Edo period, *hinaningyo* dolls were popular.

4. The first vending machines didn't come to Japan until the late 1800s or early 1900s and they only started to become popular in the 1960s. In the Edo period, people used to buy fish, vegetables, snacks, drinks and other everyday items from street sellers called *botefuri*.

5. In the picture a man is wearing denim jeans. The fashion for denim jeans didn't come to Japan until after the second world war when jeans were introduced by American soldiers. In the Edo period, men used to wear *yukata* as casual clothes.

6. In the Edo period, men would often wear *chonmage* top-knot style haircuts. The picture shows a man with a mohican or mohawk haircut. This kind of punk hairstyle didn't really become fashionable until the late 1970s and early 1980s.

7. These days skateboarding is very popular in Japan. Skateboarding began in California in the 1950s but it didn't really catch on in Japan until the early 1980s. In the Edo period, children used to play on *takeuma* bamboo stilts.

8. There were no backpacks in the Edo period. In those days, people would often carry things using *furoshiki* wrapping cloths. Originally, they were used to carry things to and from sento bath houses, but also become popular with travelers.

9. The first air conditioners for use in homes in Japan weren't developed until the late 1950s. Before that, people used to keep cool with hand fans. Also, *uchimizu*, spraying water in front of houses or stores, was a popular trick for keeping cool in the Edo summertime.

10. Traditional Japanese footwear, such as sandals made of wood or straw, was most popular in Japan until the 20th century. Men started wearing western-style footwear for business from the 1850s, but boots like the ones in the picture were not worn in the Edo period.

C Would you have liked to live in the Edo period? What are the advantages and disadvantages about life in Edo Japan?

90

WRITE   Changes

A Complete Michael's blog about life in the past and life now. Use the words from the vocabulary box below.

A lot has changed since the 1970s, but some things remain the _____. People used to listen to music on vinyl records and cassette tapes. Also, large boombox stereos became popular in the 70s and 80s with _____ people. Homes didn't have computers or the Internet at this time and there was no social media. Today people can _____ to music on youtube or download it.

Fashion has also changed a lot. In the 60s, new and exciting young designer _____ became popular and long hair was trendy. Men and women used to wear flared trousers and _____ with large collars. Though designer brands were still popular, street fashion and fast fashion became _____ in the 2020s. In the early 2020s, people also got used to wearing masks and comfortable clothes due to the coronavirus pandemic restrictions.

Food culture has changed a lot too. In the 1970s, people used to eat mostly Japanese _____. At that time, fast food and Western food had only just started to become popular as well as different kinds of Western desserts. Today, this food is still _____ but Japanese food, such as sushi and ramen remains very popular among young people.

| jackets | popular | food | trendy | brands | listen | same | young |

B Think of a period in the past, then ask an older person you know what life was like then. Ask questions about fashion, food, entertainment, sport and transport. Complete the diagram below to show how life in the past was similar or different to life today.

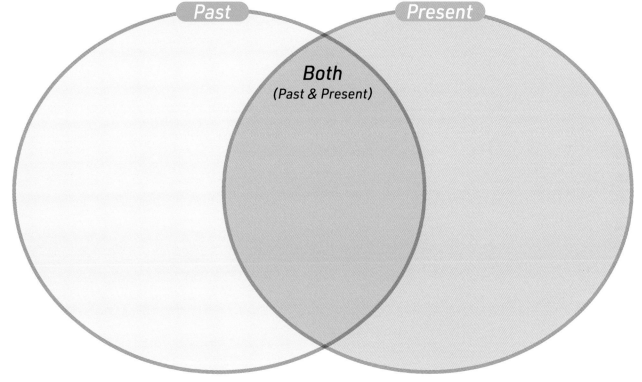

C Now write about how things have changed, or stayed the same, over time. Remember to use phrases to describe what people previously did, such as 'used to....', 'in the past' 'twenty years ago' . Also use time markers to describe what life is like now, for example, 'Today...', 'These days...', 'Nowadays...'.

Changes

VOCABULARY

DL 27   CD 27

Adjectives			
ancient *A2*	blanket *A2*	mixer	believe *A1*
antique *B2*	chores	occasion *B1*	catch *A1* on +
digital *B1*	coal *B1*	pandemic *B2*	consider *A2*
electric *A2*	collar *B1*	period *A1*	develop *A2*
portable +	coronavirus +	photography *A2*	discover *A2*
stuffed *B1*	denim *B2*	prehistoric *B2*	download *A2*
wireless	device *B1*	refrigerator *A2*	exist *A2*
	entertainment *A2*	restriction *B2*	hang *B1*
Adverbs	eraser +	smartphone +	invent *A2*
instead *A2*	electricity *B1*	spectator *B1*	remain *A2*
nowadays *A2*	evil *B2*	transport *B1*	protect *B1*
originally *B2*	finger *B1*	washing machine *A2*	punish *B1*
recently *A2*	lens +		shut *A2*
	historian *B1*	**Verbs**	spray *B2*
Nouns	image *A2*	attach *B1*	squeeze *B2*
air conditioner +	machine *A1*	ban *B2*	stream *B1*
	metal *A2*		

A Match each definition with the words on the right.

1. Something beautiful or valuable from an earlier period: _____   **a.** antique
2. Someone who studies the past: _____   **b.** catch on
3. The worldwide spread of a disease: _____   **c.** historian
4. To become popular: _____   **d.** pandemic

B Complete the table with both the verb and noun version of the words listed below.

VERB	NOUN
	restriction
protect	
	invention
punish	
	belief
develop	

C Choose the words from the box that best complete the questions. Answer the questions.

transport   protect   period   entertainment   wireless

1. What _____ devices do you often use?   A: _____
2. How do you think travel and _____ will change in the future? A: _____
3. Which historical _____ would you like to visit?   A: _____
4. How can we best _____ the environment?   A: _____
5. What is a popular form of _____ nowadays?   A: _____

D *Crossword:* Complete the crossword using the hints below.

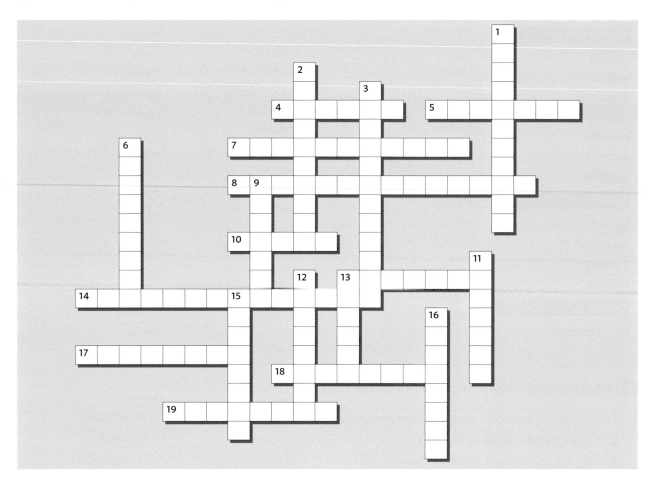

Across

4. Eating meat was _____ until the 19th century in Japan.

5. It is easy to transfer _____ images from your camera to a computer.

7.

No _____

8.

10.

13. Soccer is the most _____ sport in the world.

14.

17. Easy to carry or move around.

18. The coronavirus _____ spread around the whole world.

19.
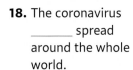

Down

1. Kyoto still has a lot of _____ townhouses known as machiya.

2.

3.

6. A person who watches something, especially a sporting event.

9.

11. We all need to do our best to _____ the environment.

12. _____, AI is becoming a more and more important part of human society.

13. In the Edo _____, people used to travel by rickshaws.

15. Alexander Graham Bell _____ the telephone.

16.

94

LANGUAGE REVIEW

Asking and answering questions about how things have changed over time.

Questions	Answers
Did you use to play soccer when you were at high school?	No, I **didn't use to** like sports when I was younger.
Didn't you use to belong to the brass band at school?	Yes, I **used to** play the trumpet. I have given up playing now, though.
What music **did you use to** listen to when you were at junior high school?	I **didn't use to** listen to music so much at school, but I love K-pop these days.
Where **did you use to** live?	I **used to** live in Miyagi prefecture before moving here.

A Complete the questions and answers using *use to* or *used to* and the appropriate verb.

1. How did you ___*use to go to*___ junior high school?

   _____*I used to go by bicycle. It took about twenty minutes.*_____

2. What TV program did you _____ when you were a child?

   _____

3. Was there any food you didn't _____ when you were a child?

   _____

4. Did you _____ in the northeast of Japan?

   _____

5. Did you _____ a uniform in high school?

   _____

6. What subjects didn't you _____ when you were at school?

   _____

B Complete the following sentences with information about how you have changed.

1. I didn't use to like _____

2. I used to be _____

3. At school, I used to play _____

4. I didn't use to be able to _____

5. After school, I always used to _____

6. My best friend used to _____

7. When I was growing up, I often used to _____ in the summer.

8. When I was a child, _____

SELF-CHECK

Write a score (1-5)* in the boxes below to show how well you can do each part of the module. If you can't do any part well, go back to the page and practice again.

* 1 : Not at all   **2 :** A little   **3 :** OK   **4 :** Well   **5 :** Very well

UNIT 11

🔍 SCAN

I can scan for information about modern devices (p.83). ································

🗣 FOCUS

I can describe how life in Japan has changed over time (p.84). ··························

👂 LISTEN

I can understand a lecture describing how life in Japan has changed over time (p.85-86). ·······································

👥 COMMUNICATE

I can read and answer statements about how the world has changed (p.87-88). ········

UNIT 12

📖 READ

I can understand descriptions about life in the Edo period (p.89-90). ·····················

✍ WRITE

I can describe changes in society over time (p.91-92). ·····································

🗨 VOCABULARY

I can understand vocabulary related to change (p.93-94). ··································

MODULE 6

Predictions

GOALS:

 Can you scan for information about the probability of events?

 Can you talk about your plans for the future?

 Can you understand a palm reading from a fortune teller?

 Can you ask and answer questions about your future plans?

 Can you understand a reading about a student's future plans?

 Can you write about your future plans?

 Can you understand vocabulary related to predictions?

MATCH

A Match the pictures 1-7 with event a-g.

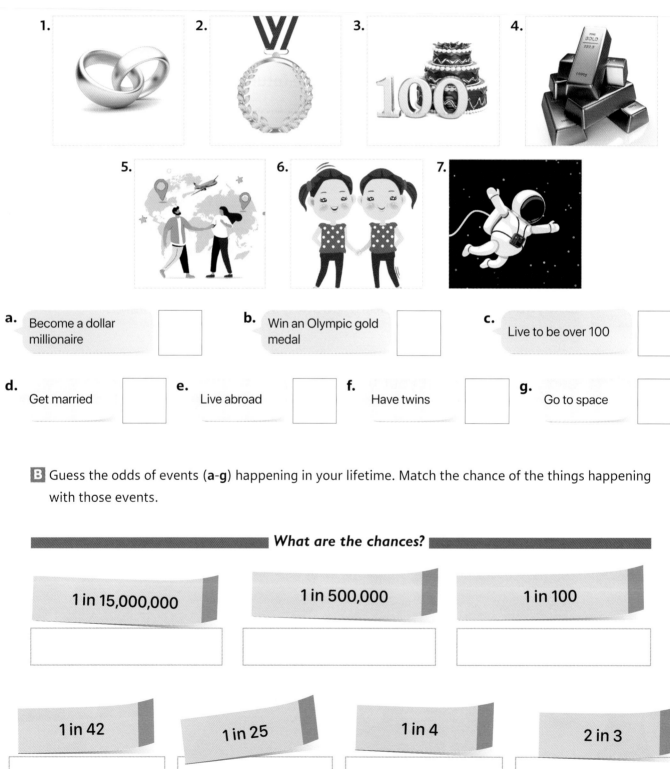

1.

2.

3.

4.

5.

6.

7.

a. Become a dollar millionaire ☐

b. Win an Olympic gold medal ☐

c. Live to be over 100 ☐

d. Get married ☐

e. Live abroad ☐

f. Have twins ☐

g. Go to space ☐

B Guess the odds of events (a-g) happening in your lifetime. Match the chance of the things happening with those events.

What are the chances?

1 in 15,000,000

1 in 500,000

1 in 100

1 in 42

1 in 25

1 in 4

2 in 3

SCAN

A *Scanning for information:* In 4 minutes, scan the texts below to find the key information. Check your answers on the previous page.

DL 28   CD 28

B Read the texts again and write the event under the correct probability on the previous page.

1.

The majority of people get married in their lifetime. Even though the number of people who remain single or live together without getting married is increasing, almost 70% of people will get married. There is a good chance that you will get married, too.

2.

Winning a gold medal at the Olympics is a great achievement. Unfortunately, hardly anyone will have this amazing experience. Fewer than 18,000 gold medals have been awarded and becoming the best in the world at any sport is extremely difficult. The odds of winning a gold medal are roughly 1 in half a million.

3.

The odds of living to be 100 years old are surprisingly good (and getting better). A lot depends on where you are from, what gender you are, as well as other factors, but about 25% of us will live to enjoy our 100th birthday cake. If you are born female in Japan today, you will have a more than 1 in 3 chance of living to be 100.

4.

If you want to become a dollar millionaire, a lot will depend on where you live and work. In America, about 3% of the population are millionaires. Worldwide, the number is about 1%, with roughly one in every one hundred people being millionaires. There are also more than 2,700 billionaires. That is about one in every 3 million people.

5.

These days, many of us travel overseas to go on vacation, but living in a foreign country is less likely. However, more and more people are now living, studying and working abroad. It is estimated that there are more than 280 million people living in foreign countries. That is a little more than 3% of the global population. That means that the vast majority of us live in the same country as we were born.

6.

About 1.6 million twins are born each year worldwide, and one in every forty two children is born a twin. The rate of twin births has risen by a third since the 1980s. There are many factors that influence whether you will have twins or not, such as age, race and family history. Japan has the lowest rate of twins in the world and Nigeria the highest.

7.

Although many children dream of becoming an astronaut in the future, there is hardly any chance that this will actually come true. Fewer than 500 people have been to space. The chance of becoming an astronaut and going to space is very low, about 1 in 15 million. It is good to dream, though.

C In pairs, discuss with your partner which of the above events you think are most likely to happen to you.

FOCUS

A Match pictures **1-12** with future events **a-l**.

1.
2.
3.
4.
5.
6.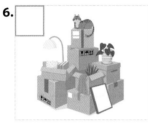
7.
8.
9.
10.
11.
12.

a. buy a new car

b. become a millionaire

c. move house

d. become fluent in a foreign language

e. become good at cooking

f. try an extreme sport

g. travel abroad

h. finish a marathon

i. learn to play a musical instrument well

j. write a book

k. work as a volunteer for a charity

l. get a full-time job

Language Focus: Probability

I may	I'm going to	I'm certain that I'll
I'm not going to	I definitely won't	I don't think I will
There's a good chance I'll	I might	I think I will
I'm sure I'll	I'll probably	I'll definitely
I doubt I'll	There's no chance I'll	I probably won't

B Complete the table below using the remaining probability expressions above.

100%	I'm going to, I'm sure I'll,
↓	I'll probably,
50%	I may,
↓	I doubt I'll,
0%	I'm not going to,

C 💬💬 *Let's talk:* With a partner, discuss the probability of the above future events happening to you in the next five years.

LISTEN Palm reading

 DL 29   CD 29

A Listen to someone having their palm read by a fortune teller. Write the name of the palm reader and put a check mark in the pictures that match the palm reading.

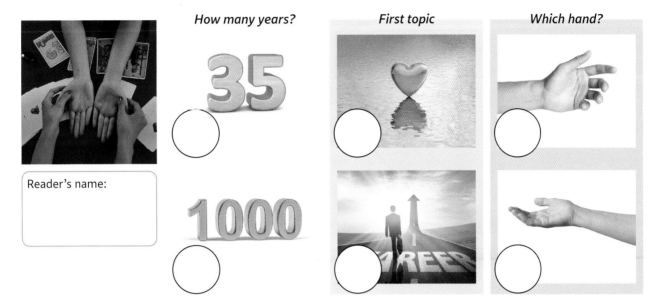

How many years?   *First topic*   *Which hand?*

35

Reader's name:

1000

B Read the palm reading below and try to guess the missing words. Then listen to the palm reading again, check your answers.

Career

I'm going to look at your head line – the center line on your palm. This shows the type of learner you are and what career you may have. Hmmm, this line is long so you are an _____ and you study hard. Well, after you graduate, you'll _____ have a job in an office. It's _____ that you'll work outside. In the future, I do see you traveling a lot though. I think you'll work in different countries and you'll eventually start your own _____ abroad. Maybe in _____ or advertising. And you're going to be very successful!

Romance

This is your heart line – the _____ line on your palm. Hmmm interesting. This line actually touches your _____ . You are lucky Neo – you're _____ going to have a happy love life. When you eventually _____ down to start your own business, you are going to meet someone and get married. And there's a good _____ you'll have a large family – I see _____ children in your family.

C Listen to the full palm reading again. Complete the mind map below with details of each topic.

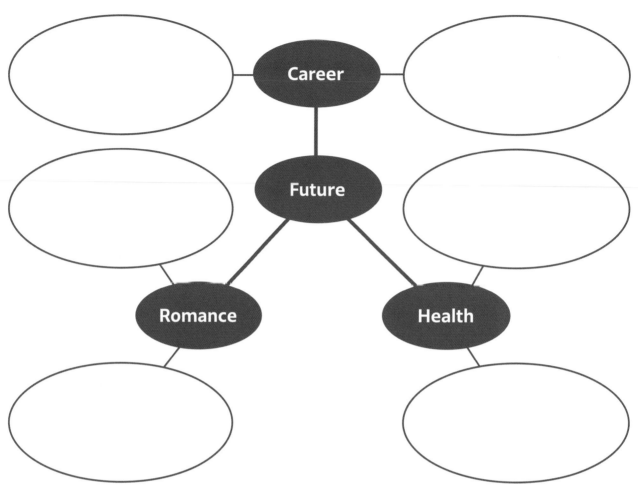

D 💬💬 Give your opinion!

1. I would like to work abroad in the future.

   Agree: _____   Disagree: _____

   Why? _____

2. My ambition is to start my own business.

   Agree: _____   Disagree: _____

   Why? _____

3. I want to have a healthily lifestyle in the future.

   Agree: _____   Disagree: _____

   Why? _____

4. I'm not planning to get married before I'm thirty.

   Agree: _____   Disagree: _____

   Why? _____

5. My career will be my main focus from now on.

   Agree: _____   Disagree: _____

   Why? _____

COMMUNICATE

What are you planning to do?

Read the questions below and write your answers to the questions. Then, think of two more questions about your future plans and answer those questions. When you have answered all the questions, ask your partner the same questions and make notes of your partner's answers.

Questions	Your answer	Partner's answer
What are you going to do this evening?		
Are you going to study English tonight?		
What do you think the weather will be like tomorrow?		
Are you planning to do anything special this Saturday?		
What are your plans for Sunday?		
Do you think you'll eat out next week?		
Are you going play sport or do any exercise next month?		
What are you planning to do in your next vacation?		
Do you think you'll travel abroad in the near future?		
What are you planning to do after you graduate?		
Do you think you will be living in the same place 5 years from now?		
What are the chances that you'll get married before you are thirty?		
How many children do you think you'll have?		

READ

Future plans

 DL 30   CD 30

A In pairs, **partner A** reads this student's future plans on this page, and **partner B** reads the same future plans on the next page. Ask your partner for hints for the missing words.

For example: **Partner A**: "Number 2".   **Partner B**: "The biggest city in West Japan".

Future Plans (A)

Career

After I ¹ **graduate**, I'm definitely going back to my hometown of ² _____ _____. My ³ **major** is Business Studies so I'll probably ⁴ _____ for a company there. I'm interested in finance, so I hope to work for an ⁵ **international** company, perhaps in banking, so that I can use my ⁶ _____ skills. I think I'll work in Japan for three or ⁷ **four** years, but I'd like to work abroad in the future. I hope I have a ⁸ _____ to do that at my company.

Family

In the future, I'd like to get ⁹ **married** but there's no chance I'll do that any time soon, though! I'm only 20 years old and I'm still at ¹⁰ _____. I guess I would also like to have a big ¹¹ **family**.

Maybe I'll have two or three ¹² _____ – boys and girls. I'm also going to have a pet because I love ¹³ **dogs**. I really like animals so that would be nice. It's unlikely I'll have a ¹⁴ _____, though. I'm ¹⁵ **allergic** to them. If possible, I really want to live near my ¹⁶ _____, as well.

Future home

As for my future home, my family lives in an ¹⁷ **apartment** in the center of the city, so one day I would like to live in a nice, big ¹⁸ _____. There's a good chance that I'll live in the ¹⁹ **countryside**. I might ²⁰ _____ to live in Japan or in an English-speaking country, like America, Canada, or ²¹ **Australia**. It would be cool to have a nice, big place there. Wherever I choose to live in the future, I definitely want somewhere with a nice big ²² _____ for my pets.

Future Plans (B)

Career

After I ¹ _____ , I'm definitely going back to my hometown of ² **Osaka**. My ³ _____ is Business Studies so I'll probably ⁴ **work** for a company there. I'm interested in finance, so I hope to work for an ⁵ _____ company, perhaps in banking, so that I can use my ⁶ **language** skills. I think I'll work in Japan for three or ⁷ _____ , but I'd like to work abroad in the future. I hope I have a ⁸ **chance** to do that at my company.

Family

In the future, I'd like to get ⁹ _____ but there's no chance I'll do that any time soon, though! I'm only 20 years old and I'm still at ¹⁰ **university**. I guess I would also like to have a big ¹¹ _____ .

Maybe I'll have two or three ¹² **children** – boys and girls. I'm also going to have a pet because I love ¹³ _____ . I really like animals so that would be nice. It's unlikely I'll have a ¹⁴ **cat**, though. I'm ¹⁵ _____ to them. If possible, I really want to live near my ¹⁶ **parents**, as well.

Future home

As for my future home, my family lives in an ¹⁷ _____ in the center of the city, so one day I would like to live in a nice, big ¹⁸ **house**. There's a good chance that I'll live in the ¹⁹ _____ . I might ²⁰ **decide** to live in Japan or in an English-speaking country, like America, Canada, or ²¹ _____ . It would be cool to have a nice, big place there. Wherever I choose to live in the future, I definitely want somewhere with a nice big ²² **backyard** for my pets.

B Complete the table below showing things that are more likely, and less likely, to happen.

100%			→ 0%
• Go back to my hometown			

WRITE

A Complete Sawa's message about her plans for the future. Use words from the vocabulary box below to help you.

Career

After I graduate from university, I think I'm going to work in _____. My major is Nursing so I'll probably work in a hospital, hopefully near Chiba city where my family lives. However, at some stage in the _____, I definitely want to study abroad again to _____ my English. I would love to spend some time living in America.

Family

I'd like to get married and _____ before I'm thirty, maybe when I am around twenty-eight or twenty-nine. I want to work and travel first though. and concentrate on my _____. I love children so I'd like to have to two kids. I don't mind if they are boys or girls. However, I want to _____ working after I have children. It would be good to live near my parents so they can help _____ of my children.

Future home

As for my future home, well, as I would like to live near my parents in Chiba city, I'll probably live in an _____ . I prefer them to houses as they are _____ to live in. I think it's unlikely that I'll live in a house, and I _____ I'll have a backyard — it would be too much trouble. I'll be busy with my job and family, so I don't think I'll have the time.

| apartment | future | settle down | take care | doubt |
| convenient | healthcare | improve | career | continue |

B What are your plans for the future? Think about your future career, family and home. Complete the diagram below using key words or examples.

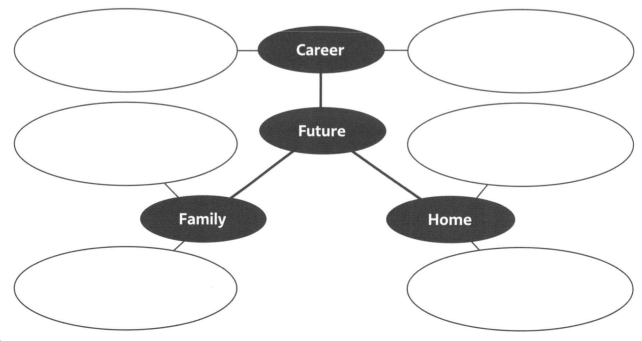

C Now write about your plans for the future. Write 3 short paragraphs about your future career, family and future home. Use your ideas from the previous page.

Future plans

VOCABULARY

Adjectives

allergic *B1* ....
global *B1* ....
likely *A2* ....
married *A2* ....
single *A2* ....
unlikely *B1* ....
vast *B1* ....
worldwide *A2* ....

Adverbs

actually *A2* ....
definitely *B1* ....
eventually *B1* ....
extremely *A2* ....

probably *A2* ....
roughly *A2* ....
surprisingly *B1* ....
unfortunately *A2* ....

Conjunctions

whether *B1* ....

Nouns

achievement *B1* ....
ambition *A2* ....
astronaut *A2* ....
backyard *B2* ....
career *B1* ....
center *A2* ....
chance *B2* ....

extreme sport *B1* ....
factor *B1* ....
finance *B2* ....
focus *B2* ....
fortune *A2* ....
gender *A2* ....
healthcare *B2* ....
influence *A2* ....
intellectual *B2* ....
majority *B1* ....
millionaire *B2* ....
odds *B2* ....
palm *B1* ....
population *A1* ....
prediction *A2* ....

probability *B1* ....
rate *B1* ....
space *B2* ....
twin *A1* ....

Verbs

concentrate *A2* ....
continue *A2* ....
depend *A2* ....
doubt *B2* ....
estimate *B1* ....
improve *A2* ....
remain *A2* ....
rise *B1* ....
settle down + ...
take care of + ...

A Match each definition with the words on the right.

1. More than half the total number or amount: _____
2. The number of people living in a country, area, or place: _____
3. Relating to the whole world; worldwide: _____
4. A person who has been trained for traveling in space: _____

a. astronaut
b. population
c. majority
d. global

B Complete the list using opposites of the words listed.

unlikely ⟷ _____likely_____

majority ⟷ _____

remain ⟷ _____

rise ⟷ _____

continue ⟷ _____

married ⟷ _____

C Choose the words from the box that best complete the questions. Answer the questions.

> millionaire   achievement   influence   improve   fortune

1. Which person has had a positive [ ] on you?   A: _____
2. How would you like to [ ] yourself?   A: _____
3. Would you like to become a [ ] ?   A: _____
4. What has been your greatest [ ] so far?   A: _____
5. Have you ever been to a [ ] teller?   A: _____

D *Crossword:* Complete the crossword using the hints below.

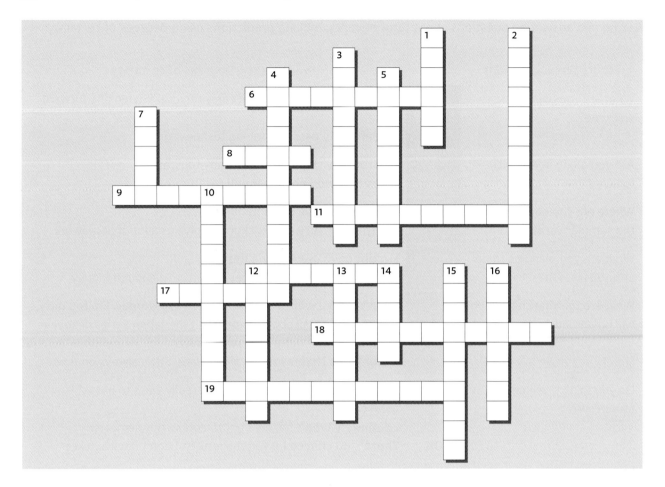

Across

6.

8.

9. It is _____ that there will be almost 10 billion people living on Earth by 2050.

11. The _____ of Japan is about 125 million.

12.

17.

18. The _____ of that happening is quite high.

19.

Down

1.

2. Something that a person has completed successfully.

3. Saying what you think will happen in the future

4. A very educated person

5.

7.

10.

12.

13. My English has _____ a lot this year.

14. To not be sure about something.

15. I will _____ pass the test. I'm 100% certain.

16. It is _____ that it will rain tomorrow. I think it will be sunny.

LANGUAGE REVIEW

Asking and answering questions about future events, making predictions using degrees of certainty.

Future tense questions		Predictions – Degrees of certainty
What are you doing this weekend?	100%	My mother **is going to** cook curry tonight. I'm looking forward to it. **I'll definitely** pass my driving test next time.
Are you going out to eat tonight?		**I'll probably** stay home and study tonight. **There's a good chance it will** rain tomorrow.
Where are you going to spend the summer vacation?		**I think I will** have pasta for lunch. **I'm (pretty) sure** the teacher **will** give us a lot of homework.
What are you planning to do after this lesson?	50%	I **might** go to see a movie this weekend. I **may** go abroad this summer if I can save enough money.
What are the chances that you will go abroad next year?		**I don't think** I **will** be able to go out this Saturday. I'm too busy. Hiroshima Carp **probably won't** win the Japan Series next year. **I doubt I'll** have more than two children. **It's unlikely that** my friend will be late. She's always on time.
Do you think it will rain tomorrow?		I'm **not going to** be absent again. I really want to pass this course. **I definitely won't** fail my English course this semester.
	0%	**There's no chance I'll** win the lottery. I don't have a ticket!

Complete the following sentences with information about yourself.

I'm going _____ this weekend.

I'll definitely _____ next year.

I'll probably _____ tonight.

What's the weather going to be like tomorrow?

There's a good chance it will _____ tomorrow.

I think I will have _____ for dinner tonight.

I'm (pretty) sure _____ this summer.

I might _____ next year.

I may be able to _____ after I graduate from

university, if I _____ .

I don't think I will _____ on Sunday.

I probably won't _____ today.

I doubt I'll _____ this month.

It's unlikely _____

I'm not going to _____ this year.

I definitely won't _____ ever again.

There's no chance _____ !

MODULE 6 SELF-CHECK

Write a score (1-5)* in the boxes below to show how well you can do each part of the module. If you can't do any part well, go back to the page and practice again.

* 1 : Not at all   **2 :** A little   **3 :** OK   **4 :** Well   **5 :** Very well

UNIT 13

SCAN

I can scan for information about the probability of events (p.99). ....

FOCUS

I can talk about my plans for the future (p.100). ....

LISTEN

I can understand a palm reading from a fortune teller (p.101-102). ....

COMMUNICATE

I can ask and answer questions about my future plans (p.103). ....

UNIT 14

READ

I can understand a reading about a student's future plans (p.104-105). ....

WRITE

I can write about my future plans (p.106-107). ....

VOCABULARY

I can understand vocabulary related to predictions (p.108-109). ....

PROJECT E   Which group enjoys change more?

Ask 10 classmates (divided into two different groups of 5, such as males and females) to give their opinion.

	Group 1	Group 2
1. When I cut my hair.....	Number of respondents	
a. I like to keep the same hairstyle that I have had for a long time. (**1 point**)		
b. I sometimes change my hairstyle. (**2 points**)		
c. I like to try different hairstyles. (**3 points**)		
Total:		
2. When I watch movies.....	Number of respondents	
a. I enjoy watching the same movies that I used to watch when I was younger. (**1 point**)		
b. I sometimes watch movies that I used to watch when I was younger. (**2 points**)		
c. I like to watch movies that I haven't seen before. (**3 points**)		
Total:		
3. When I go on holiday....	Number of respondents	
a. I like to go to the same place that I used to go when I was younger. (**1 point**)		
b. I sometimes like go to places that I used to go when I was younger. (**2 points**)		
c. I always like to go to different places. (**3 points**)		
Total:		
4. When I go to my favorite restaurant.....	Number of respondents	
a. I almost always choose the same food. (**1 point**)		
b. I sometimes choose the same food. (**2 points**)		
c. I like to try different kinds of food. (**3 points**)		
Total:		
5. After I graduate, I would like to live and work....	Number of respondents	
a. in the same place all my life. (**1 point**)		
b. in two or three different places. (**2 points**)		
c. in more than three different places. (**3 points**)		
Total:		
6. Trying new things makes me feel:	Number of respondents	
a. Nervous (**1 point**)		
b. A little unsure (**2 points**)		
c. Excited (**3 points**)		
Total:		

RESULTS

Complete the charts below with the scores from the previous page.

	Group1	Group2	Group1	Group2	Group1	Group2	Group1	Group2	Group1	Group2	Group1	Group2
15												
14												
13												
12												
11												
10												
9												
8												
7												
6												
5												
	Question 1		Question 2		Question 3		Question 4		Question 5		Question 6	

For example: *If a group mostly chooses (c's), then they enjoy trying new things. They like change in their life!*

If a group mostly chooses (a's), then they don't like change. They like the same routine.

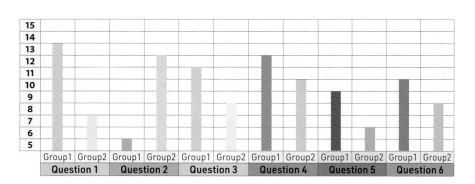

REPORT

Write up the results of your survey. Explain how the groups feel about change.

For example: *The people in Group 1 like to try different hairstyles more often than the members of Group 2. Almost everyone in the Group 1 chose the answer "c", and their total was 13 points. However, only one member of Group 2 chose the answer "c", and their total, 8 points, was much lower.*

PRESENTATION

Take turns explaining the results of your survey on the previous page.

PROJECT F

What are the future goals of your classmates?

Ask 10 students the questions in the table below about their future plans. Find out reasons for their answers.

	Student 1	Student 2	Student 3	Student 4	Student 5
What job do you want after you graduate?					
What do you want to be doing ten years from now?					
Do you want to get married and have children in the future?					
Where would you like to be living ten years from now?					
What is your future dream?					

	Student 6	Student 7	Student 8	Student 9	Student 10
What job do you want after you graduate?					
What do you want to be doing ten years from now?					
Do you want to get married and have children in the future?					
Where would you like to be living ten years from now?					
What is your future dream?					

REPORT

Write the results of your interviews and give your opinions about them. Use the vocabulary page to help you.

For example: *Six students want to work abroad for an international company. They want to use their language skills in their future career.*

PRESENTATION

Take turns explaining the results of your interviews using the answers from the previous pages.

Image Credit and Sources

Framework English B (CEFR A2-B1)

CEFRの評価基準で学ぶ４技能 B (CEFR A2-B1)

2024年1月20日　初版第1刷発行
2024年2月20日　初版第2刷発行

著　者	Tim Woolstencroft
	Colin Thompson
発行者	福　岡　正　人
発行所	株式会社　金　星　堂

（〒101-0051）　東京都千代田区神田神保町 3-21
Tel　（03）3263-3828（営業部）
（03）3263-3997（編集部）
Fax　（03）3263-0716
https://www.kinsei-do.co.jp

編集担当　長島吉成　　　　　　　　　　　Printed in Japan
印刷所・製本所／株式会社カシヨ
本書の無断複製・複写は著作権法上での例外を除き禁じられています。
本書を代行業者等の第三者に依頼してスキャンやデジタル化することは、
たとえ個人や家庭内での利用であっても認められておりません。
落丁・乱丁本はお取り替えいたします。

ISBN978-4-7647-4201-7　C1082

MODULE

SELF-CHECK

for submission

MODULE 1 SELF-CHECK

Write a score (1-5)* in the boxes below to show how well you can do each part of the module. If you can't do any part well, go back to the page and practice again.

* 1 : Not at all   **2 :** A little   **3 :** OK   **4 :** Well   **5 :** Very well

UNIT 1

SCAN

I can scan for information about people's biography (p.7). ⋯⋯⋯⋯⋯⋯⋯⋯⋯⋯⋯⋯ ☐

FOCUS

I can ask and answer personal questions (p.8). ⋯⋯⋯⋯⋯⋯⋯⋯⋯⋯⋯⋯⋯ ☐

LISTEN

I can understand a conversation about studying abroad (p.9-10). ⋯⋯⋯⋯⋯ ☐

COMMUNICATE

I can ask and answer detailed personal questions (p.11). ⋯⋯⋯⋯⋯⋯⋯⋯⋯ ☐

UNIT 2

READ

I can understand a biography about Albert Einstein (p.12-13) ⋯⋯⋯⋯⋯⋯ ☐

WRITE

I can write my own biography (p.14-15). ⋯⋯⋯⋯⋯⋯⋯⋯⋯⋯⋯⋯⋯⋯⋯ ☐

VOCABULARY

I can understand vocabulary related to biographies (p.16-17). ⋯⋯⋯⋯⋯⋯ ☐

ID:＿＿＿＿＿＿＿＿＿＿＿   Name:＿＿＿＿＿＿＿＿＿＿＿＿＿

MODULE 2 SELF-CHECK

Write a score (1-5)* in the boxes below to show how well you can do each part of the module. If you can't do any part well, go back to the page and practice again.

* **1:** Not at all   **2:** A little   **3:** OK   **4:** Well   **5:** Very well

UNIT 3

SCAN

I can scan for information about people's personalities (p.23). ·································

FOCUS

I can ask and answer questions about likes, dislikes, abilities and personalities (p.24). ····

LISTEN

I can understand a job interview for a flight attendant (p.25-26). ·····························

COMMUNICATE

I can answer detailed questions about likes and abilities (p.27-29). ··························

UNIT 4

READ

I can read and understand information about star signs (p.30-31). ····························

WRITE

I can write about my likes, dislikes, abilities and personality (p.32-33). ····················

VOCABULARY

I can understand vocabulary related to personalities (p.34-35). ······························

ID:＿＿＿＿＿＿＿＿＿＿＿＿   Name:＿＿＿＿＿＿＿＿＿＿＿＿＿＿＿

MODULE 3 SELF-CHECK

Write a score (1-5)* in the boxes below to show how well you can do each part of the module. If you can't do any part well, go back to the page and practice again.

* 1 : Not at all   **2 :** A little   **3 :** OK   **4 :** Well   **5 :** Very well

UNIT 6

SCAN

I can scan for information about famous places in Japan (p.47). ⬜

FOCUS

I can recommend places to visit in Japan (p.48). ⬜

LISTEN

I can understand recommendations for places to visit in Kyushu (p.49-50). ⬜

COMMUNICATE

I can answer general knowledge questions about Japan (p.51). ⬜

UNIT 7

READ

I can understand tourism advertisements about Hokkaido (p.52-53). ⬜

WRITE

I can write an advertisement for a place I know well (p.54-55). ⬜

VOCABULARY

I can understand vocabulary related to Japanese culture (p.56-57). ⬜

ID: _____   Name: _____

MODULE 4 SELF-CHECK

Write a score (1-5)* in the boxes below to show how well you can do each part of the module. If you can't do any part well, go back to the page and practice again.

*1: Not at all　　2: A little　　3: OK　　4: Well　　5: Very well

UNIT 8

🔍 SCAN

I can scan for information about recipes (p.63). ·· [ ]

🎧 FOCUS

I can describe how to cook something (p.64). ····································· [ ]

👂 LISTEN

I can understand cooking instructions to make a pie (p.65-66). ············· [ ]

👥 COMMUNICATE

I can describe Japanese food (p.67-68). ·· [ ]

UNIT 9

📖 READ

I can understand instructions on how to make French toast (p.69). ········· [ ]

✏️ WRITE

I can write cooking instructions for a food dish (p.70-71). ················· [ ]

🗨️ VOCABULARY

I can understand vocabulary related to cooking (p.72-73). ·················· [ ]

ID: _____　　Name: _____

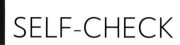

MODULE 5 SELF-CHECK

Write a score (1-5)* in the boxes below to show how well you can do each part of the module. If you can't do any part well, go back to the page and practice again.

* 1 : Not at all   **2 :** A little   **3 :** OK   **4 :** Well   **5 :** Very well

UNIT 11

SCAN

I can scan for information about modern devices (p.83). ⋯⋯⋯⋯⋯⋯⋯⋯⋯

FOCUS

I can describe how life in Japan has changed over time (p.84). ⋯⋯⋯⋯⋯⋯

LISTEN

I can understand a lecture describing how life in Japan has changed over time (p.85-86). ⋯⋯⋯⋯⋯⋯⋯⋯⋯⋯⋯⋯⋯⋯⋯⋯⋯⋯

COMMUNICATE

I can read and answer statements about how the world has changed (p.87-88). ⋯⋯⋯

UNIT 12

READ

I can understand descriptions about life in the Edo period (p.89-90). ⋯⋯⋯⋯⋯

WRITE

I can describe changes in society over time (p.91-92). ⋯⋯⋯⋯⋯⋯⋯⋯

VOCABULARY

I can understand vocabulary related to change (p.93-94). ⋯⋯⋯⋯⋯⋯

ID: _____   Name: _____

Write a score (1-5)* in the boxes below to show how well you can do each part of the module. If you can't do any part well, go back to the page and practice again.

* 1 : Not at all   **2 :** A little   **3 :** OK   **4 :** Well   **5 :** Very well

UNIT 13

SCAN

I can scan for information about the probability of events (p.99). ·····························

FOCUS

I can talk about my plans for the future (p.100). ·······························

LISTEN

I can understand a palm reading from a fortune teller (p.101-102). ·····················

COMMUNICATE

I can ask and answer questions about my future plans (p.103). ·······················

UNIT 14

READ

I can understand a reading about a student's future plans (p.104-105). ·····················

WRITE

I can write about my future plans (p.106-107). ····································

VOCABULARY

I can understand vocabulary related to predictions (p.108-109). ·························

ID: _____   Name: _____